I0807742

Praise for

Real Marriage Made Simple

"Dr. Chris Thurman has invested decades in helping couples strengthen their marriages. Rather than offer quick-fix solutions grounded in worldly wisdom, he has been faithful to point people to the scriptures for ultimate guidance and counsel. Whether you're engaged, newly married, or have been married for decades, *Real Marriage Made Simple* will be a much-needed tool to build a healthier marriage. I highly recommend it!"

—**Vicki Courtney,** bestselling author of *Rest Assured, 5 Conversations You Must Have with Your Daughter*, and *5 Conversations You Must Have with Your Son*

"Dr. Chris Thurman cuts through the noise to deliver timeless wisdom in *Real Marriage Made Simple*. With clear insights and practical steps, this book is for every couple who wants to strengthen their connection and navigate marriage with grace and intention."

—**Drs. Les & Leslie Parrott,** *New York Times* bestselling authors of *Saving Your Marriage Before It Starts*

"For years I have turned to the writings of Dr. Chris Thurman for wisdom and insight regarding managing relationships. On earth there is no more important relationship than that of a husband and wife. So, Chris is my go-to when trying to help married couples navigate the storms of life. His compassionate approach and solid principles will help any marriage move in the right direction. Simply put, we cannot have a healthy, loving marriage if we are unwilling to play by the principles that can take us there. If you are looking for practical principles to make your marriage thrive, you have just found the answer in *Real Marriage Made Simple*."

—**Dr. Tom Hufty,** Senior Pastor, First Baptist Church, Maryville, Illinois

"Dr. Chris Thurman is a wise and insightful guide on how to live life fully and deeply. *Real Marriage Made Simple* is an important book that helps couples develop a closer, more loving bond. It is full of practical wisdom on how marriages can flourish as husbands and wives love one another in a way that glorifies God. I highly recommend it."

—**Phil Christensen,** Senior Pastor, Southwest Bible Church, Austin, Texas

"We have been blessed to have Dr. Chris Thurman teach at our church for over thirty years, helping countless couples improve their marriage. *Real Marriage Made Simple* is the culmination of his efforts to take biblically solid principles and apply them to strengthening the marital bond between a husband and a wife. If your marriage is in a season of turmoil or stagnation, the simple principles in this book will guide you to a healthier relationship. I highly recommend it to you as a valuable resource to help couples experience the healthy and loving relationship God intends them to have."

—**Dr. Matt Cassidy,** Senior Pastor, Grace Covenant Church, Austin, Texas

"In his new book, *Real Marriage Made Simple*, Dr. Chris Thurman draws from experience and a God-given calling to help couples have a loving marriage that lasts a lifetime. Chris's answers are simple to do but costly to the soul and require a deepening relationship in both the marriage and with God. Therein lies the most significant value of this book . . . it is practical advice rooted firmly in biblical truth. This is not a book for those who want to improve their spouse. Instead, it is sincere truth that first responds to God's Word to 'see if there be any hurtful way in me,' as the psalmist declared. It follows with such deeply rooted antidotes for healing that every couple, marriage group, and church community will find a go-to for marriages that seek the path to move forward. Forty years of counseling, writing, and mentoring have been written down so that every marriage, no matter the age or condition, can change . . . if the 'want to' is there! I highly recommend this book!"

—**Dennis Gallagher,** Pastor at Large, Freedom Fellowship Church, New Braunfels, Texas

"Dr. Chris Thurman's latest book, *Real Marriage Made Simple*, equips husbands and wives with practical tools and handles to make actual marriages thrive and flourish. With his typical grace, honesty, and humor, Chris encourages and challenges couples to build a marriage that fulfills both their hopes and responsibilities. This book will be an invaluable resource in the local church, and we highly recommend it!"

—**Mac and Julie Richard,** Pastors, Lake Hills Church, Austin, Texas

"Combining humor, concrete examples, and helpful advice, Dr. Chris Thurman's new book, *Real Marriage Made Simple*, provides much-needed wisdom for navigating the highs and lows of marriage with love and grace. Every husband and wife who read this book will see their reflection in its pages and learn new skills to strengthen their union. Don't read Dr. Thurman's words only to learn new information but to change unhealthy habits and leave a better legacy for future generations!"

—**Keith Ferguson,** Lead Pastor, Cityview Bible Church, Round Rock, Texas

Real Marriage Made Simple

Proven Principles for Thriving Together

DR. CHRIS THURMAN

LEAFWOOD PUBLISHERS
an imprint of Abilene Christian University Press

REAL MARRIAGE MADE SIMPLE

Proven Principles for Thriving Together

LEAFWOOD
PUBLISHERS
an imprint of Abilene Christian University Press

ISBN 978-1-68426-323-3 | LCCN 2024950400

Printed in the United States of America

Cataloging-in-Publication Data is on file at the Library of Congress, Washington, DC.

Cover design by Greg Jackson, Thinkpen Design
Interior text design by Sandy Armstrong, Strong Design

Leafwood Publishers is an imprint of Abilene Christian University Press
ACU Box 29138
Abilene, Texas 79699

1-877-816-4455
www.leafwoodpublishers.com

25 26 27 28 29 30 31 // 7 6 5 4 3 2 1

Dedicated to couples who want to thrive, not just survive

I love being married. It's so great to find that one special person you want to annoy the rest of your life.

—Rita Rudner

Contents

Introduction

I like things to be simple. It is why I like playing checkers more than chess, especially against my elementary school-aged granddaughters who I regularly crush. For me, chess is just way too complicated.

Marriage is a lot like chess. Actually, it is more like three-dimensional chess. Marriage is a complex, maddening mix of personality differences, family of origin issues, developmental stuckness, human fallenness, spiritual blindness, and a hundred other things that make it the most challenging and difficult of all relationships. Anyone who says marriage is simple, much less easy, has either never been married or is still on their honeymoon.

I wrote *Real Marriage Made Simple* to try to take some of the complexity out of marriage. In this book, we are going to explore ten time-tested relationship principles God has given us for how to interact with our spouse. If we comply with these principles, our marriages are going to be pretty good, maybe even great. If we refuse to go along with them, we are going to be unhappily married and may even start looking for a way out.

While I wrote this book for couples to use on their own, I primarily wrote it for small group use. I believe in the biblical notion, "As iron sharpens iron, so one person sharpens another" (Prov. 27:17). I encourage you to find other couples to go through this book with you so you can sharpen each other into having better marriages than you ever thought possible.

I am a firm believer in putting what you learn into practice, so I have included a workbook. The Bible says, "Do not merely listen to the word, and so deceive yourselves. Do what it says" (James 1:22). For each chapter, there is a corresponding lesson in the workbook that will help you put what you learn into action. Please, make sure you do the workbook along the way so you will get the most out of reading this book.

Since marriage is a serious matter, I tried to keep the book lighthearted. Please do not interpret that as me not taking marriage seriously. I take marriage *very* seriously. My stabs at humor are an effort to keep the mood of the book light and upbeat as we cover one serious topic after another.

Marriage is complicated. No book, seminar, or sermon is ever going to make that less true. Nevertheless, I hope *Real Marriage Made Simple* helps you see the core relationship principles of marriage more clearly so you and your spouse can treat each other in a kind and loving manner that brings greater glory to God.

Thank you for reading this book. I hope you find it helpful. I believe reading a book like this shows you are serious about your marriage and want it to be all that God wants it to be. That is a wonderful thing, and I applaud you for it. I will be praying for you.

Blessings,
Chris

PART ONE

KEEPING MARRIAGE SIMPLE

CHAPTER ONE

Can't We Just Get Along?

The most important single ingredient in the formula of success is knowing how to get along with people.

—Theodore Roosevelt

If it is possible, as far as it depends on you, live at peace with everyone.

—Romans 12:18

There is an old joke that there are three rings in marriage—the engagement ring, the wedding ring, and suffering. Yes, I know, that is a bad joke. Unfortunately, it has a lot of truth to it.

Most of us enter marriage with high expectations for how well we are going to get along and the walking-on-sunshine level of closeness we are going to experience. While we do the best we can to create a loving bond with our spouse, our efforts often come up well short of what we hoped for. At that point, many of us disconnect from our spouse and become two ships unhappily passing in the night, wondering if there is any hope we might come back together in a kind, compassionate, and loving way.

Maybe you feel that way about your marriage. Maybe you entered your marriage thinking about how great it was going to be, only to find that things did not turn out quite like you expected. Maybe you feel emotionally and spiritually disconnected from your spouse and wonder if the two of you will ever experience the kind of closeness that led you to walk down the aisle. If so, this book is for you.

God came up with the idea of marriage. And because he did, God gets to make the rules for what it takes to have a healthy, loving relationship with each other. If we play by his rules, we are going to end up with something enjoyable, even exciting. If we thumb our nose at them, we are going to end up with something painful, even intolerable. When it comes to having a thriving marriage, it is God's way or the highway.

I wrote this book to help couples better understand God's most important relationship principles for having a healthy marriage. Far too many couples are either unaware of these principles or aware of them but unwilling to live by them. Having been married for forty-four years and counseled hundreds of couples during my five decades as a psychologist, I can tell you these principles work when applied. I can also tell you that we have to make them a daily part of our interactions with our spouse if we want to experience a truly loving marriage.

Throughout this book, I am going to take you into my counseling office to give you a feel for the struggles many couples experience in marriage. The couples I mention are composites of the people I have worked with over the years. I do this to protect their identities and safeguard the confidentiality that is crucial to them being able to do good work in counseling. Let me take you into a fairly typical opening session with a couple whose marriage has become a painful place of anger, despair, and hopelessness.

Every Couple's Battle: Following God's Principles for a Healthy Marriage

Kevin and Courtney had been married for twenty years and had three teenage children when they first came to see me. They had put marital counseling off as long as possible, choosing instead to go on the occasional weekend marriage retreat put on by their church in an effort to jump-start their relationship.

Kevin and Courtney genuinely loved each other and were committed to staying married, but they were deeply discouraged by how badly things were going between the two of them. Proverbs 13:12 says, "Hope deferred makes the heart sick, but a longing fulfilled is a tree of life." When Kevin and Courtney first came to see me, their hearts were "sick" in that the hope they had for a healthy, loving closeness had been deferred for a long time.

"How can I help?"

"Dr. Thurman, we've grown apart over the years . . . The pressures of having our careers and trying to raise three kids at the same time has been challenging, to say the least. Lately, it seems like our relationship has gotten worse. Our fights are more frequent, and neither of us really seem to want to be around each other," Kevin responds.

"Is that how you see it, Courtney?"

"Yes, for the most part," she replies.

"For the most part?"

"I don't think Kevin is being totally honest about just how bad our fights have been lately," she answers.

"How bad have they been?"

"Well, they've involved lots of yelling, sometimes with hateful name-calling thrown in for good measure," Courtney answers.

"That cuts both ways. You've yelled at me just as much as I have at you," Kevin defensively jumps in.

"I wasn't suggesting otherwise . . . I'm just saying I think you're minimizing how bad things are between us. We aren't going to make any progress in here if we aren't honest about how badly you treat me," Courtney fires back.

"How badly I treat you! Wow, that's the pot calling the kettle black! Why don't you point that finger back at yourself?" Kevin answers.

"Every time I talk about my issues, you use them against me. You throw them back in my face and use them to run from your own. I don't feel safe enough to be open with you about my flaws. If you're waiting for me to do that with you, you're going to wait a long time," Courtney responds.

"So are you. Not only do you use my struggles against me, you never forgive me for anything I've done. You bring things up from before we even got married and rub them in my face. How safe does that make me feel?" Kevin argues back.

"I would forgive you if you would stop doing the things you know hurt me. Since you don't, I know you're not really sorry and you're going to do them again. You only have yourself to blame for why I don't forgive you," Courtney answers.

"Oh, so it's my fault you're unforgiving," Kevin defensively replies.

"Pretty much . . . I'm not going to forgive you if you keep doing the same hurtful things over and over. No one in their right mind would do that," Courtney responds.

"I've changed over the years . . . I'm not the same guy I used to be," Kevin says, pleading his case.

"You haven't changed! You're the same guy I married twenty years ago. All you do is focus on yourself and what you need! You don't care what I and the kids need," Courtney lashes back.

"I resent that! I bust my hump all day to put a nice roof over your head," Kevin angrily responds, masking the hurt he feels that Courtney said what she did.

"Kevin, I don't need you for that! I can do that for myself! I need you to meet my emotional needs, not my survival needs," she answers.

"Well, no wonder you don't appreciate anything I do! Don't think I haven't noticed," Kevin replies.

"It's hard to appreciate what you do when I never get what I want in this marriage. You give to me the way you want to give, not the way I need you to," Courtney fires back.

"Courtney, you never focus on any of your issues in our marriage. To hear you tell it, I'm always the one who's an insufferable jerk . . . I'm always the one hurting you. I can't begin to tell you how many times you've been hurtful to me. And to make matters worse, you never apologize, which means you either don't think you ever do anything wrong, or you're just too prideful to admit it," Kevin responds, firing the last salvo.

"Let me jump in here for a minute. I would imagine the two of you have had this argument a thousand times and that nothing good ever comes out of it. In fact, it only serves to drive you further apart. Am I right so far?" I ask.

"Yes," Courtney answers.

"You got that right," Kevin chimes in.

"I believe I know what is causing the two of you to fight so much and disconnect from each other," I suggest.

"Really? What?" Courtney asks.

"Yeah, what are we doing wrong?" Kevin asks.

"I don't think you're doing it intentionally, but there are nonnegotiable principles for getting along well with your spouse that the two of you are not complying with. Every time you violate one of these principles, you trigger each other into feeling hurt and angry. Until you understand what these principles are and make them a part of your daily interactions, your marriage can't help but be a wounding, painful place," I offer.

"What are they? What are these principles you're talking about?" Kevin asks.

"I'm not ready to go into them today, but I would be happy to help you work on them in the weeks and months to come, if you're willing. So, here's your first homework assignment. I want the two of you to go home and talk about this session. I want you to decide if you want to work with me to repair your relationship. And even though you don't know what they are yet, I want you to decide if you're going to put your marriage under the authority of these relationship principles or keep putting your marriage under your own authority for how you interact. If you are willing to do the former, I would be happy to work with you. If you want to keep doing the latter, I will be happy to give you a referral to another counselor," I reply.

Kevin and Courtney did what I asked. They talked things over, prayed about it, and came to the decision that they were going to see me for marital counseling. We spent the next six months laboring together to help them better understand the core biblical principles for a thriving marriage and make them a daily part of how they interacted with each other.

I have great admiration for couples like Kevin and Courtney. They worked hard, humbled themselves before God and each other, stopped presuming to live by their own misguided principles for marriage, and overcame a lot of the conflict and hurt they were experiencing. Not only did the frequency of their fights significantly decrease, but they began to experience more warmth and tenderness toward each other. No couple ever gets to a place of marital nirvana, at least not on this side of heaven, but Kevin and Courtney did a really good job of repairing the damage they had caused each other and became a healthier and more loving couple.

It is not a pipe dream to say we can have the marriage we always wanted, but we have to cooperate with God and get real about what it takes to get there. God has graciously provided the relationship principles that can get us to the land of marital milk and honey, but we have to implement them if we want to make it to such a wonderful place.

May I Lower the Bar in Marriage While Actually Raising It?

We marriage counselors have a pretty high standard for the level of closeness (attachment, intimacy, bonding, connection, togetherness) we want couples to attain. We challenge couples to aspire to have a *deeply intimate, safe, cherishing, joy-filled, and loving bond* with each other and not settle for anything less. And this is appropriate, given that marriage is the only "one flesh" (Mark 10:8) relationship we have on earth.

But at the risk of you thinking I am howling at the moon crazy, I believe the standard of a deep, intimate closeness with our spouse is beyond our reach if we do not comply with the principles we explore in this book. Simply put, we cannot have a healthy, loving marriage if we are unwilling to play by the principles that can take us there.

Let me use a tennis analogy to drive this home. Let's say someone is really upset that they do not play tennis very well, and they go see a tennis coach to get some help. After watching them hit some balls for a few minutes, a competent tennis coach can see pretty quickly why they are not playing well—they are trying to hit the ball with the handle of the racquet, not the strings. Until this person complies with a core principle of tennis—"Hit the ball with the strings, not the handle"—they are never going to play well. In fact, they are going to play badly and lose every time they step out on a court.

This is what is going on in most marriages. Couples go to marriage counseling because they are not getting along well, and they are understandably upset about it. A competent marriage counselor can see pretty quickly that a couple is not getting along because they are not complying with basic relationship principles for how to be close to their spouse. Metaphorically speaking, the couple is trying to hit the ball with the handle of their racquet and not the strings. A big part of a marriage counselor's job is to help a couple better understand what these core principles are and get them to start complying with them so they can experience a loving marriage.

The insanity of many marriages is that couples keep hitting the ball with the handle of their racquet and expecting to get along well with each other. They keep doing the same unhealthy things over and over, all while expecting a different (better) result. This is why so many couples feel their marriage is driving them crazy. When we keep interacting with each other outside of God's principles for how to thrive in marriage, we *are* driving each other crazy.

In light of this reality, may I suggest we temporarily *lower* the bar in marriage by simply working to comply with the basic principles required for *getting along* with our spouse. If you think that is not much of a challenge, think again. Each of the principles we explore in this book are simple in theory but hard to do in practice. If you are like me, you will spend the rest of your marital life needing to get better at complying with these principles, and you will not feel you lacked enough of a challenge for what it takes to grow into a more loving spouse.

Everybody wins in marriage when we stop focusing on having a deep, intimate closeness with each other and start practicing the principles that can get us there. Whether we realize it or not, most of us have been hitting the ball with the handle in marriage, not the strings. We have been unknowingly violating God's principles for how to treat each other, and we keep getting the same bad, painful result. This has to be turned around if we want to have the marriage God wants us to have, a marriage that goes beyond what we could have ever hoped for or imagined.

Some Final Thoughts

What I hope you have heard so far is that there are certain nonnegotiable principles governing marriage that determine how well or poorly we get along with our spouse. If we comply with these principles and our spouse does as well, our marriage will be reasonably good and enjoyable, even great. If either spouse refuses to practice these principles, marriage is going to be a painful, destructive dumpster fire where no one feels safe, peaceful, or loved.

While this may be hard to hear, we violate *all ten* relationship principles we cover in this book, and we do it a lot more often than we realize. We are all too fallen to come anywhere close to being perfect when it comes to living according to these principles. Consequently, none of us can *honestly* puff out our chest and be proud about how we treat our spouse.

As you read this book, try to avoid focusing on how your spouse violates the principles we are going to explore. It will be hard for you not to think about your spouse being the more egregious rule breaker in your marriage, but I encourage you to avoid doing that. If you really want to grow, apply these principles *to yourself* and be humble about the fact that on your best day as a spouse, you struggle to practice them at a high level.

Do not shame or condemn yourself that you struggle to live by these principles. If it is any comfort to you, this is a common problem among we married folks. The fact that we find it difficult to consistently comply with these principles is not to be used as a battering ram against our sense of self. We are fearfully and wonderfully made in the image of God and worthy of love, and we are never to tear ourselves or our spouse down just because we are left-footed when it comes to getting along with each other (my apologies to left-footed people). As you read this book, allow yourself to come under *conviction* not *condemnation* that you find it hard to live by these principles, and stay committed to getting better at applying them to your marriage over time.

Finally, do not try to have a better relationship with your spouse in your own power. I have never found my self-empowered efforts to love my wife to be enough. For me, God's love and grace working in me and through me is the only way I have been able to treat her well over time. God is the only one who has the power to help us live by these principles. Do yourself a favor and ask him to help you practice these principles so they become your day-to-day way of lovingly interacting with your spouse.

With no further ado, let's explore ten biblical principles for developing a close, loving bond with our spouse. Practice them as best you can with God's help, and you will find yourself getting along better with your spouse than you ever thought possible.

And, please, after you finish each chapter, go to the workbook and do the corresponding lesson there. Well, what are you waiting for?

PART TWO

PROVEN PRINCIPLES FOR THRIVING TOGETHER

CHAPTER TWO

Stay in Your Own Backyard

Judging others makes us blind, whereas love is illuminating. By judging others we blind ourselves to our own evil and to the grace which others are just as entitled to as we are.

—Dietrich Bonhoeffer

Why do you look at the speck of sawdust in your brother's eye and pay no attention to the plank in your own eye? How can you say to your brother, "Let me take the speck out of your eye," when all the time there is a plank in your own eye? You hypocrite, first take the plank out of your own eye, and then you will see clearly to remove the speck from your brother's eye.

—Matthew 7:3–5

An elderly couple had been shopping at a grocery store, and the wife decided to steal a can of peaches. The inevitable happened and she was caught. Upon her court date, the judge asked her what she had stolen.

"Your Honor, I stole a can of peaches."

The judge replied, "How many peaches were in the can?"

She said, "Six."

The judge then said, "I will sentence you to six days in jail."

Her husband stood up behind her and replied, "Your Honor, she also stole a can of peas."

As a marriage counselor, it is obvious to me there is a serious problem in how this husband approached his wife. Rather than stay in his own backyard, he focused on how she had stolen not only a can of peaches but a can of peas. Apparently, he wanted her to spend more than just six days in jail paying for her crime.

Rather than look at why he was trying to get his wife in more trouble than she was already in, this particular husband was eagerly trying to secure more jail time for her. He jumped the fence into his wife's backyard, saw her as the more troubled of the two of them, and tried to get the judge to send her to jail for a longer period of time. What the husband was unwilling to see is that he was the more noticeably flawed of the two of them, given that he would do such a mean thing to his wife.

You may think I am overinterpreting this story, but I think not. Even though it is meant to be humorous, there is nothing funny about a husband or a wife being unwilling to stay in their own backyard, someone who focuses on their spouse's flaws and defects rather than their own. Focusing on what is flawed and defective about your spouse while being oblivious to the things that are flawed and defective about yourself is a sure prescription for marital disharmony and disconnection.

Most people find it difficult to stay in their own backyard and focus on *their* flaws as a human being. It is a common human malady for us to be in significant denial about *our* issues, all while having an unhealthy fixation on the defects in others. I cannot think of a single client coming to see me about their marriage who opened with, "Doc, I'm here to focus on *my* flaws as a spouse. I'm a mess, and I desperately need your help so I can love my spouse better!" Seriously, I would fall out of my therapist chair if I ever heard anyone say that.

What I have heard more than a few million times is, "Doc, I'm here to tell you about what a horrible person my spouse is and see if you can help me get them to change." If I wanted to keep my practice full, I would reply, "I'm game—let's talk about how awful your spouse is and see what we can do to help them get their act together." What I say instead, often at the expense of a full schedule, is, "Hey, I know you are hurting, and we are certainly going to talk about your spouse at times, but I'm only willing to work with you if you focus on your own issues and make some changes that will keep you from being part of the problem." Some people cannot fly out of my office fast enough when I say that.

The majority of us focus on the defects in others, especially the people who have wounded us the most deeply. While I certainly have empathy and compassion for how my clients have been hurt by their spouse, I am not going to do them much good if I let them camp out in their spouse's backyard the whole time I am working with them.

Let's go back into my counseling office to drive this home.

The Husband Who Camped Out in His Wife's Backyard

Ben met his wife, Sally, while both were in college. They dated for a couple of years but decided to go their separate ways when Sally graduated a year ahead of Ben. Both went off and found success in their respective careers; Ben as a home builder and Sally as a graphic designer. After a few years, they got back in touch when Ben contacted Sally on Facebook. They started dating again, and they got married a year later.

At our first meeting, Ben described his marriage to Sally as okay, certainly not awful by any stretch of the imagination. But a number of things over the years had begun to bother him about Sally, and he was in my office to talk about them and get some help for how to handle their relationship better.

The primary lightning rod for Ben's anger toward Sally was her spending habits. Ben admitted Sally was not overspending in any significant way, but he felt she played a little too fast and loose with the money they earned as a couple. Ben wanted "objective, third-party input" on what he should do about not only this issue but other things bothering him about his wife.

"It just makes me want to pull my hair out when I come home at the end of a long day and see shopping bags and Amazon packages on the kitchen table. It's all I can do to not blow up at Sally about the way she spends money."

"How do you react?"

"I usually mutter something under my breath, like, 'I can see they had another sale at Nordstrom's today—thanks for saving us so much money!'"

"How does Sally respond when you talk to her that way?"

"She usually fires back with something equally sarcastic."

"Like?"

"Oh, she'll say something like, 'I don't see you stopping yourself from getting stuff at Home Depot every time you're there. The garage is full of tools you never use.'"

"Is that true?"

"Well, yeah, but what's that got to do with her being one of Nordstrom's favorite customers? And why does she think it's okay to talk to me like that?"

"Well, I'm just curious, why do you think she talks to you like that?"

"Obviously, she doesn't like that I think she spends too much and feels the need to remind me I do the same thing."

"Does she?"

"Does she what?"

"Does she need to remind you that you spend just as much money as she does?"

"Doc, are you on my side or not? I can get this abuse at home!"

"Very funny. Are you being sarcastic with me right now?"

"Yeah. Sorry. Obviously this is frustrating the heck out of me."

"I get that, Ben, and I hope you understand I have compassion for both you and Sally about this issue in your marriage."

"Compassion for her! She's the one spending us into an early grave! Why would you have compassion for her?"

"Because she's married to someone who won't stop focusing on *her* issues with money while turning a blind eye to his own."

"If I wanted Dr. Phil for a counselor, I would have tried to get on his show!"

"Well, unfortunately, you're stuck with me. Plus, Dr. Phil wouldn't see someone like you because you're too easy of a case."

"I'm just upset with how much money my wife spends and that she won't admit it, and I want to know what to do about it."

"Okay, here's my advice for what to do about it—focus on your own spending habits. Work on reining in that part of you that bought three power tools last month, none of which you've ever used. Try focusing on what is going on inside of you when you go to a place like Home Depot, walk the aisles for hours, and buy things you don't need. Ben, if you will focus on your own spending issues, you'll be modeling something for Sally that just might inspire her to look at why she has ten pairs of running shoes in her closet, many of which she has never worn. If you don't start with yourself and how you spend money, you aren't going to make very much, if any, progress with her."

"But . . . but . . ."

"Ben, there's no 'but' to what I'm saying. If you won't look at your own spending habits in the marriage, Sally is going to keep getting defensive and will fire back at you for being a hypocrite. She isn't going to trust that your intentions are good when you bring her issues up, nor should she. Sally needs a husband who will face his own stuff, not one who focuses on what's wrong with her."

"But that's no fun! It's a lot more enjoyable to get on Sally about how Nordstrom keeps raising her spending limit because they love her so much!"

"I'll grant you that focusing on her issues is a lot more enjoyable, but it isn't helping your marriage. In fact, it's causing pretty serious problems between the two of you. I know you don't want that. I know you love Sally and want to get along better with her. It's been painful to both of you that you've drifted apart over the years, and I know you miss how close you were when you first got married."

"I do . . . we haven't been close for a long time now. She knows it, too. Neither of us seems to know how to bridge the gap between us."

"Well, if it's any comfort to you, drifting apart is common in marriage. I'm just trying to help you see that a major reason there is distance between the two of you is that you use her struggles to run from your own. If you will stay focused on your own problems, I think Sally will find that motivating and feel a lot safer to be around you."

"I can't argue with your logic. I'm definitely going to need your help on this . . . I've spent a lot of years grinding my teeth about her spending habits and all the other things she does that bother me."

"You've got my help, Ben. You know that. We'll work on this together. I'm optimistic it will make your relationship with Sally better."

This is what Ben and I did. I gave him the simple yet challenging assignment of talking about his issues in his marriage to Sally. He was always free to talk about what Sally did that *triggered* his frustration, but I stopped him any time he would home in on her flaws and use them to run from his own. Ben got a lot better at staying out of Sally's backyard and focusing on his own issues in life, and his relationship with Sally began to improve as a result.

We say in counseling that when one person in a relationship changes, the other person tends to change as well. That is what Ben found out in his marriage to Sally. He discovered that when he focused on his own issues, his wife felt safer to face her own. This is one of the most important ways we all need to change in marriage—take our eyes off our spouse's flaws and put them squarely on our own.

The Four Types of "Stay in Your Own Backyard" Spouses

I want to take you into the four types of spouses we can be in marriage related to staying in our own backyard, three of which are unhealthy and lead to a damaged and disconnected marriage. After you look these over, ask yourself if you tend to fall into one particular category more often than the others.

The Peeping Tom/Thomasina

This spouse can be found peering over the marital fence and looking at all the weeds in their spouse's backyard. Rather than focus on their own defects, this spouse focuses on their partner's flaws and what a mess they are as a human being.

The Fence-Jumper

This spouse is not content to simply peer over the fence to look at their partner's defects. They jump the fence, stomp around in their spouse's stuff, point out all the things that are wrong with them, and give their spouse all kinds of unsolicited feedback before returning to their own backyard.

The Camper

This is the worst marital style of all. Not only does this spouse jump the fence between their issues and their partner's issues, but they never leave. They stay in their spouse's backyard and emotionally bully them into admitting to all their flaws and defects. They set up their tent and all their camping gear in their spouse's issues and spend the rest of the marriage demanding that they change.

The Homebody

This spouse is doing it right. Sure, on occasion, they peer over the fence and focus on their spouse's issues. They may even jump the fence on occasion if they get upset enough about their spouse's flaws. But for the most part, this spouse is humbly aware he or she has more than enough defects to focus on for the rest of their life, and they spend the majority of their time in their own backyard working on their own stuff.

The first three kinds of spouses are unwilling to spend time facing their own issues because doing so is too threatening and painful. They use their spouse's issues to run from their own. In doing so, they communicate to their spouse that there is no need to spend any time working on their own stuff because they are dang-near perfect.

Given that all of us have lots of flaws, the three styles of being an unhealthy spouse are always harmful to a marriage. It is never okay to use someone else's defects as a way to run from our own. And most of the time, the things we do not like about our spouse are those things that we struggle with ourselves.

If we are going to get along better with our spouse, we need to resist the urge to peer over the fence and zero in on what is wrong with them. We certainly need to restrain ourselves from jumping the fence and criticizing them for being a noticeably imperfect human being. And for goodness' sake, let's never pitch our tent in our spouse's backyard and emotionally bully them into getting their act together.

The "Stay in Your Own Backyard" Marriage

Whether or not you comply with the "stay in your own backyard" principle is important in determining how well or poorly you and your spouse get along.

For a couple to truly feel safe, each person has to spend the majority of their time focusing on their own defects. Each spouse needs to know they are married to someone who is humble enough to focus on their own flaws rather than what they do not like about their partner. If this is not understood and lived out in marriage, no one feels safe or that it is okay to be an imperfect, messed-up human being. No one can be healthily and happily married to a person who runs from their own defects by focusing on their partner's shortcomings.

All this raises an important question: What are we supposed to do when we don't like something about our spouse? If it isn't okay to *focus* on their flaws, much less critically bring those flaws to their attention, are we just supposed to stuff our feelings and keep them to ourselves? Are we just supposed to "grin and bear it" in marriage when our spouse's shortcomings show up and negatively affect us?

The simple answer is no. We will go into this question in greater depth in a later chapter, but for now there is a simple guideline for what to do when you run into a flaw or defect in your spouse that is upsetting or hurtful to you. When your spouse acts in a way that you believe to be wrong or inappropriate, take a deep breath and ask yourself the following question: "What do I need from my spouse that I'm not getting?" Resist the urge to focus on their behavior and shift your focus to what you need from them that you're not receiving. Let me give you an example.

Let's say your spouse has been stressed out about work and ignored you for weeks. The natural tendency in a lot of marriages would be to bring this to their attention in a critical or demeaning way, like, "You've been totally ignoring me for weeks, and I'm sick of it." In situations like this, I want you to figure out what you are needing from your spouse and, rather than be critical about it, put your hurt and anger in the form of a request. Humbly say something like, "I know you have been stressed out lately about work, but I miss spending time with you and would like to spend some time with you tonight. Would you be willing to do that?"

Do you see how different that is? Instead of criticizing or attacking your spouse, you are channeling your hurt and anger into a request so that the relational need not being met (in this case, attention) can be addressed. Your spouse, whether they decide to give you attention or not, at least will not feel attacked and will be more likely to meet your need. Either way, you stayed out of their backyard, remained in your own, figured out what you needed that you were not getting, asked for it like a mature adult, and moved the relationship forward.

I challenge my couples to "Channel hurt and anger into a request." They are often pleasantly surprised by how things begin to turn around when they do. Not criticizing your spouse but simply letting them know what you need can radically change your marriage. When you practice this different way of handling your hurt and anger, you learn how to quit focusing on the things that are wrong with your spouse and become more aware of what you need from them that you are not getting. This is a major paradigm shift for most couples. Those couples who get good at doing this are amazed at how much of a change it makes in their marital relationship and how safe and loved everyone starts to feel.

Some Final Thoughts

There is something quite shocking about a person who fundamentally stays in their own backyard and focuses on their own issues. Quite shocking. I want to challenge all of us who are married to be shocking in this way. I want to challenge us to stop focusing on how messed up our spouse is and noncondemningly focus on our own messed-upness.

This one change can make a huge difference in marriage. Every couple I have worked with who was willing to stay in their own backyard saw their marriage improve. There is something about humbly addressing our own flaws and channeling our hurt and anger into a request that takes a lot of pressure off of a marriage and allows everyone to take a deep breath and relax.

Please, do not use your spouse's flaws to run from your own. Stay in your own backyard, focus on what needs to change about you, and channel your hurt and anger in marriage into a humble request. You will be doing everyone a favor, and your marriage will noticeably improve over time.

CHAPTER THREE

Own Your Own Stuff

The day you graduate from childhood to adulthood is the day you take full responsibility for your life.

—Jim Rohn

Then the man and his wife heard the sound of the LORD God as he was walking in the garden in the cool of the day, and they hid from the LORD God among the trees of the garden. But the LORD God called to the man, "Where are you?" He answered, "I heard you in the garden, and I was afraid because I was naked; so I hid." And he said, "Who told you that were naked? Have you eaten from the tree that I commanded you not to eat from?" The man said, "The woman you put here with me—she gave me some fruit from the tree, and I ate it." Then the LORD God said to the woman, "What is this you have done?" The woman said, "The serpent deceived me, and I ate."

—Genesis 3:8–13

A woman's husband had been ill in the hospital for several months. He kept slipping in and out of a coma, but she remained faithfully by his bedside every single day.

Then one day, when he woke from his coma, he motioned for her to come nearer to him. As she moved closer and sat beside him, eyes filling with tears, he whispered into her ear, "You know what? You've been with me through all the tough times. When I got fired from my job, you were there to support me. When my business failed, you were there for me. When I got shot, you were by my side all the time. When we lost the house, you stayed right here with me. And even when my health started failing, you were still by my side. You know what?"

"What, dear?" she asked gently, smiling as her heart began to fill with warmth, her eyes welling with tears.

He said, "I think you're bad luck."

You are probably starting to think I cannot let a story be funny without using it to make an important point about marriage. You'd be right. Here, we have another problem that negatively impacts pretty much every marriage on the planet—the unwillingness to own your own stuff.

Funny as it is, the husband in this story was blaming his wife for all his problems, as if she were an unlucky penny he picked up along the way. He was acting as if she had done nothing but cause him trouble throughout the marriage. Rather than take responsibility for his own role in getting fired from his job, his business failing, someone shooting him, them losing the house, and his health failing, it was all his wife's fault because she was this ever-present dark cloud over his head that caused all these bad things to happen to him.

The tendency to blame your spouse for your stuff goes all the way back to the Fall, of course. No sooner had Adam and Eve taken a bite out of an apple than they were blaming someone else for having done so. Adam blamed two people that day—God and Eve. Eve blamed one—the serpent. I could be wrong on this, but that strikes me as biblical evidence men are sicker than women. But I digress.

We are prone to making two mistakes when it comes to taking appropriate responsibility in marriage. One is to take too much, and the other is to take too little. We psychologists call the former "neurotic" and the latter "character disordered." Through no fault of our own, we come into the world as little ones both neurotic and character disordered in how we view the issue of taking responsibility. Unfortunately, even after we get older, we continue to do the same thing, especially in marriage.

Every day of marriage, we are fighting an internal war between our neurotic and character disordered sides. Sometimes we take too much responsibility, and sometimes we take too little. Some days we think, "Everything is my fault," and some days we think, "Everything is my spouse's fault." Neither style helps us to achieve a healthy, loving relationship.

Let's take a trip inside my counseling office to see how a couple was damaging their marriage by blaming their feelings and actions on each other rather than taking full responsibility for both.

The Blame Game Couple

Jack and Debbie, both attorneys, had been married for twelve years when they came to see me. Their marriage was an emotionally painful battleground, each person firing off salvo after salvo aimed at criticizing and demeaning the other. Mostly for their children's sake, they decided to stay married no matter how emotionally destructive they were to each other. While there were many moving parts to why they had such a bad marriage, the biggest was that neither one of them would take responsibility for their feelings and actions when it came to how they interacted.

"I am sick and tired of Jack blaming me for how unhappy he is in the marriage. All he does is complain about the fact that I never give him enough of what he needs and that it's why he is so miserable," Debbie says, firing the opening shot in what was our ninth counseling session.

"That's rich . . . you constantly blame me for why you stomp around the house angry and why you isolate yourself in the bedroom all the time," Jack fires back.

"I do not!" Debbie angrily responds.

"You do, too!" Jack replies, just as angry.

"Let me interrupt for a second," I interject, jumping in a lot sooner than I usually do. "Is it possible that what the other is saying about you is true?"

"What? You think I blame Jack for being unhappy?" Debbie asks, not wanting to hear an honest answer.

"Yes, I do. And I think Jack blames you for how unhappy he is in the marriage. It's one of the common themes in many marriages . . . It's all your fault I'm miserable, and if you would just treat me better, I'd be happy as a bird with a french fry," I reply.

"That's not true," Jack replies, unwilling to look honestly at what I said.

"Sure it is," I reply, standing my ground. "Everybody, to some degree, blames their spouse for how they feel and how they act."

"That's not true," Jack responds, as if I didn't hear him the first time.

"Jack, be honest with me. When someone's riding your bumper in traffic, isn't there a part of you that blames them for the fact that you feel angry and pump your brakes to make them back off?" I ask.

"No," he digs in.

"Not even the smallest part of you?" I suggest.

"No," he digs in even further.

"Jack, I don't think you're being honest with yourself. It's common for all of us to blame our anger, anxiety, sadness—even our happiness and joy—on others as if they were the cause of these feelings, when they actually come from inside us."

"You don't think the other person has anything to do with what we feel?" Debbie asks, getting her foot in the door of our discussion.

"No, I didn't say that. What I'm saying is that people *trigger* us to feel and act the way we do, not *cause* our feelings and actions," I answer.

"Doc, you're splitting a pretty fine hair there, aren't you?" Jack says, taking the discussion back over.

"Yes, I am, but in relationships, especially marriage, it's a hair we need to split for things to go well. If we don't split that particular hair, all we're going to do is play the blame game and feel bitter and resentful, and the relationship is going to go in the tank," I argue.

"Why?" Debbie asks. "Why is this so important?"

"Because nobody in their right mind is going to tolerate others blaming them for what they feel and how they act. It's hard enough to take responsibility for our own emotions and actions, much less allow someone else to pile theirs on top of us. Don't you agree?" I ask, hoping they will.

"I agree with you in principle, but nobody looks at things the way you're talking about," Jack replies, sounding like the lawyer he is.

"Jack, I wouldn't say nobody, but I agree that very few do. But I can tell you the road to ruin in marriage is paved with people blaming their feelings and actions on their spouse," I respond to my argumentative lawyer-client.

"Doc, wouldn't you agree that a spouse is responsible *to some degree* for how their actions impact the other?" Debbie asks, sounding like the lawyer she is.

"No," I respond, keeping it short and not so sweet.

"No?" she responds, confusion written all over her face.

"No. And since both of you are lawyers, let me make my case. Would you agree that people respond quite differently at times to the same event . . . like when they're at a football game and a team scores a touchdown? Aren't some fans happy while others are upset?" I argue.

"Yes, but I don't see where you're going with that," Jack replies.

"Where I'm going is this: How is it that people respond differently to the same event if the event caused their reaction? How did a touchdown scored cause one fan to be happy and another to be angry?" I ask, feeling like the best lawyer in the country.

"I think I'm beginning to see your point," Debbie concedes. "The same event can't cause different reactions. The difference in reactions has to do with the differences in the people watching the game."

"Exactly," I agree.

"But what does all this have to do with marriage?" Jack asks, still in fight mode and wanting to defeat the argument I'm making.

"It has everything to do with marriage. If you won't admit your reactions to each other reflect how *you* view things, you are going to keep making each other the culprit in why you're so unhappy. Hasn't that been what your marriage is all about . . . attacking the other person for doing things that 'upset' you?" I ask, knowing the answer to the question.

"You're right about that . . . all we seem to do is spew anger at each other and pull away into our separate worlds until the next fight starts," Jack agrees, beginning to soften a little.

"Look, I care too much about the two of you to let you blame each other for your unhappiness in marriage. I'm going to challenge you every time we're together to express what you feel without blaming the other for why you feel it. The path you've been on is the path to the destruction of your marriage. You need to head in a whole new direction where you let each other know how you feel without blaming them for those feelings."

I am happy to say Jack and Debbie accepted my challenge. They worked hard to take responsibility for their emotions and actions in their marriage. I taught them to use "I feel" language rather than "You made me feel" language. I also taught them to fight constructively rather than destructively about the hurtful things going on between the two of them. They both agreed to stop participating in the blame game, take full ownership of their feelings and actions, and stop playing the victim card when talking about feeling hurt and angry in their relationship.

The Three Kinds of "Blaming" Marriages

I mentioned earlier that people make two mistakes when it comes to taking responsibility in marriage. One is to take too much, which is neurotic. The other is to take too little, which is character disordered. I want to quickly run you through how these two inappropriate styles of taking responsibility often interact in marriage.

The Character Disordered–Character Disordered Marriage

In this marriage, both spouses blame the other for their feelings and actions. No one is taking responsibility for their own stuff. It sounds something like this.

"It's your fault I ripped a door off a hinge because you made me mad when you forgot to pick up my dry cleaning."

"Well, it's your fault I forgot to pick up the dry cleaning because you didn't remind me, so you only have yourself to blame."

The Character Disordered–Neurotic Marriage

In this marriage, one spouse blames the other for how they feel and act, and the other spouse accepts all the blame. One spouse is taking too little responsibility, and the other is taking too much. It sounds something like this.

"It's your fault I ripped a door off a hinge because you made me mad when you forgot to pick up my dry cleaning."

"You're right. Not only is it my fault I forgot to pick up your dry cleaning, but I'm fully responsible for you responding by ripping a door off the hinge. I apologize for both."

The Neurotic–Neurotic Marriage

In this marriage, both spouses take responsibility not only for their own feelings and actions (as they should) but for the other person's feelings and actions as well. It sounds something like this.

"Sweetheart, it's my fault you forgot to pick up my dry cleaning because I forgot to remind you. And I'm really sorry I so grossly overreacted by ripping a door off a hinge. I hope you will forgive me."

"Nothing to forgive you for, dear. It's my fault you ripped a door off a hinge when I forgot your dry cleaning because I made you mad. Please forgive me for forgetting the dry cleaning and making you so mad."

These three marital styles are all dysfunctional in that they involve taking too much and too little responsibility in the midst of conflict, and these unhealthy styles of interacting cannot take you to a healthy marriage. Sadly, far too many couples bounce back and forth between these three styles of interacting with each other, causing their relationship to be even more confusing and crazy-making.

The only marital style that works when it comes to taking appropriate responsibility involves both people owning their own emotions and actions. This is a ***Responsible–Responsible Marriage,*** and it sounds something like this.

"Sweetheart, it was wrong of me to rip a door off a hinge when I found out you forgot my dry cleaning. That was immature, and I want to apologize. Me acting that way had nothing to do with you, and I'm truly sorry I did that. Please forgive me. I will keep working on my temper so that you don't feel you have to walk around on eggshells anymore."

"Sweetheart, thanks for apologizing . . . I really appreciate it. I accept your apology and forgive you. I'm sorry I forgot your dry cleaning, and that's on me. I will try to remember to do better in the future."

A Responsible–Responsible Marriage is uncommon, but Oh! It is a sight to behold! It is what you see when two full-fledged adults are interacting with each other rather than two children. Conflict is resolved more quickly and cleanly, the couple is able to enjoy the times in between ruptures more deeply and freely, and they are freed up to move on to the next source of conflict in the relationship that is inevitably coming their way.

Any marriage counselor worth their salt is going to help couples move out of the three destructive styles of interacting and into a constructive Responsible–Responsible style so the marriage can grow into a safe and loving place.

The "Owning Your Own Stuff" Marriage

If there is to be a healthy, intimate bond in our marriage, we have to get into a regular habit of practicing the Responsible–Responsible style of owning our own stuff. Let me give you a few pointers on how to do this.

First, you must make an internal commitment to take full responsibility for your emotions and actions in marriage. You have to go "all in" when it comes to seeing your life this way. A half-baked commitment to owning your own stuff just won't cut it.

Second, you must become more aware of when you blame your feelings and actions on your spouse and not put them in the position of having to point it out. A lack of self-awareness about this issue is destructive in marriage, and far too often we do not even realize we are blaming our spouse for our stuff.

Third, while it is important to be self-aware, ask your spouse to point out when you blame them for your stuff. Be courageous enough to let them tell you when you fall into the blame game. Try not to get defensive or counterattack.

Fourth, when you realize you have blamed your spouse for your feelings and actions, or they point out that you have done it, apologize. Say something like, "I want to apologize that I blamed you for what I was feeling and how I acted, and I hope you will forgive me for doing that. That's not the kind of spouse I want to be. I'm sorry I did it, and I want you to know I'm working hard to get out of that pattern with you."

Fifth, start using "I" language in your interactions with your spouse. The goal here is not to stuff your feelings about what your spouse does and does not do, it is to own those feelings and the actions that go with them. Instead of saying, "You made me mad when you showed up thirty minutes late for our dinner date, and that's why I had two glasses of wine before you arrived," say, "I felt angry when you showed up thirty minutes late for our date and made a bad choice to drink too much before you arrived." All that may sound like semantics, but it is not.

Finally, see this issue and all the others we cover in this book as a challenge to become a more mature adult. What I mean is that blaming your feelings and actions on others is what children do, not what mature adults do. Realize that blaming your spouse for your own stuff is a reversion back to childhood, something you do not want to do. Marriage is God's main way of helping us grow up, and all the principles we cover in this book will help you become a more mature adult if you practice them on a regular basis.

Some Final Thoughts

Having been a marriage counselor for a good while, I can assure you that unless a couple is willing to do the two things we have explored so far—stay in their own backyard and own their own stuff—their marriage is going to be a mess. Keep in mind that the principles of a godly marriage do not adjust to us. We have to comply with them if we want to grow closer and thrive as a couple. No matter how hard it is to practice these principles, it is worth the effort because of the wonderful results waiting for us down the road.

Before closing, I want to say one other thing about the issue of taking responsibility in marriage. Even though we are not responsible for our spouse's feelings and actions, we are supposed to care about them. Let me explain.

Any loving husband would *care* that he forgot his wife's birthday and that she feels hurt by it. He would not hide behind, "Well, according to the experts, you're responsible for what you feel, so don't put your hurt on me!" We will talk about it more in a later chapter, but we need to have empathy and compassion for what our spouse feels and how they act, even when we think they are overreacting or should not be reacting at all. Let me exaggerate this to make the point.

Let's say I actually remember my wife Holly's birthday, get her a dozen roses, take her to the finest restaurant in town, and cap it all off by flying her to Paris for the week and booking a two-night stay at the Palace of Versailles. Let's say, for some unknown reason, Holly is furious with me that I went to all that effort to celebrate her birthday. Even in a situation like that, I need to care that she is upset, listen deeply to her expressing it, and see what I can do to get us back on the same page of marital harmony and happiness.

Yes, in marriage, each spouse is responsible for what they feel and how they act. At the same time, we are supposed to genuinely *care* about what our spouse feels and how they act, even when their feelings and actions do not make much sense to us. We will talk about this more in the chapter on compassion, but I want to make sure we never lose sight of having a caring heart toward our spouse when they react to the things we do.

Okay, enough said. You're still doing the workbook, aren't you?

CHAPTER FOUR

Give More Than You Take

My father said there were two kinds of people in the world: givers and takers. The takers may eat better, but the givers sleep better.

—Marlo Thomas

It is more blessed to give than to receive.

—Acts 20:35

A man and his wife were having some problems in their marriage and were giving each other the silent treatment.

The next week the man realized he would need his wife to wake him at 5 a.m. for an early morning flight to Chicago. Not wanting to be the first to break the silence, he finally wrote on a piece of paper, "Please wake me at 5 a.m."

The next morning the man woke up, only to discover it was 9 a.m. and he had missed his flight. Furious, he was about to go and see why his wife hadn't woken him when he noticed a piece of paper by the bed. It said, "It's 5 a.m., wake up."

When we experience conflict in marriage, it is not uncommon for us to stop meeting each other's needs, especially our spouse's psychological needs (which include acceptance, affection, affirmation, appreciation, attention, comfort, encouragement, respect, security, support, and understanding). The willingness to meet our spouse's psychological needs often goes flying out the window when we feel wounded, and marriage can become a painful "hurt people hurt people" kind of relationship.

That is what is happening in this story. The problems this couple were having in their marriage were tied to not doing a good job of meeting each other's psychological needs, and they had fallen into a destructive way of coping with it—the silent treatment. When the husband left his wife a note asking her to wake him at 5 a.m., he was putting his need for support in play. When the wife wrote him a note saying it was 5 a.m. and to get up, she was being passive-aggressive and getting him back for not meeting her needs prior to all this happening.

We live in a world where far too many people's styles of interacting with others is "What's in it for me?" These kinds of people are usually on the prowl for what they can take from others, and they often leave people feeling drained and exploited. Fewer in number are the people whose interaction style is "What's in it for you?" They are typically looking for how to give to others and usually leave people feeling refueled and loved. The "What's in it for me?" people take until others have little left to give. They then move on to a fresh supply source to get more. The "What's in it for you?" people do not go from one supply source to the next because they *are* a supply source and trust that people will ultimately give back to them.

These two kinds of people stand out when looking back over human history. Some do nothing but take from others to fulfill their narcissistic needs for power, possessions, and pleasure. Adolf Hitler comes to mind. Others do nothing but selflessly give to others to meet their spiritual, psychological, and physical needs. For me, the best example of that person is Jesus Christ.

To get along with our spouse, we have to give more than we take. If we want to have a healthy competition with our spouse in marriage, we need to see who can out-give whom in terms of meeting each other's legitimate relational needs. If we win that competition, we will get along reasonably well, our spouse will want to be around us, and they will cry buckets of tears when we die. If we lose that competition and take more from our spouse than we give, our marriage will not be very good, we will get along horribly, and our spouse will probably dance on our grave.

A Husband Always on the Take

Beth and Sam, a couple in their early forties, had been married for just a few years when they first came to see me. Both had been married before and brought teenage children into their marriage. Beth was a bank executive, and Sam was a wealth management advisor.

Even though they had just been married for a short time, they were both miserable for different reasons. Sam was miserable because he felt Beth did not attend to his needs very well, and Beth was miserable because she felt Sam was a bottomless pit of needs who did not really care about meeting her needs in return.

"Dr. Thurman, I just can't do it anymore. I'm forty-two years old and have two high school daughters, two high school stepsons, a stressful job, and an overly demanding husband who never wants to hear the word no," Beth states with an exasperated and exhausted tone in her voice.

"That's not fair! I can hear a no, I just think it's all you ever say to me," Sam responds.

"You've got to be kidding! I say yes to your needs a hundred times for every time I say no," Beth responds, slightly exaggerating.

"You're constantly saying no to me, and even when you say yes, you do it begrudgingly," Sam answers.

"That is simply not true. All you ever seem to do around the house is ask me to serve you—get me this, bring me that, take care of this for me. Would it kill you to ask what you can do for me?" Beth shoots back.

"So, this is all on me, is it? I'm the reason you're unhappy," Sam replies, not really caring if he is.

"You're not listening to what I'm saying. I'm trying to tell you that a major reason I'm unhappy is that it always seems to be about what you want from me. I feel used and exploited. I feel like you're there for you, not for me. Is it really a shocker I'm unhappy?" she responds, holding her ground.

"Man, I must be an extremely selfish guy," Sam sarcastically answers.

"Whether you want to see it that way or not, I think you *are* selfish when it comes to our marriage. I think you are only interested in getting your needs met, and you don't really care about me and what I need. That's not okay. You can't take and take and take and expect me to be the kind of wife who's happy and wants to be around you," she responds.

"Well, you make that clear every day," Sam says.

"Let me jump in here," I cut in, hoping to steer the conversation in a productive direction. "Sam, not to pile on, but I think Beth is trying to tell you something you need to hear. I think she is trying to tell you she has a lot on her plate, feels everyone demanding things from her all the time, and feels that you aren't looking out for what she needs from you."

"Dr. Thurman, I think that's a gross mischaracterization of our marriage and, frankly, I'm angry she would say that about me in front of you. I'll admit, I'm as selfish as the next guy, but I'm not some insatiable sponge who can never get enough from my wife," he answers.

"Sam, I don't think that's the issue here. I don't think the issue is whether or not you ask for too much. I think the issue is whether or not you're thinking about her and what she might need from you. Are you?" I ask.

"Well, it's not like I don't think about her at all . . . I do . . .," he replies.

"That's not what I'm asking. I'm asking whether, on a regular basis, you're thinking about what she needs from you. Is that foremost on your mind?" I ask.

"No, not foremost on my mind, but it's there somewhere," he answers.

"I appreciate your honesty. I think if you're going to make any progress in the marriage, Beth's needs are going to have to be as important as your own. I'm not saying you shouldn't put your needs in play. I'm just saying that before you do, you might want to make sure you're thinking about her. Until that shift takes place in your heart, I don't think you're going to find that Beth wants to be around you all that much," I suggest.

I spent some individual time with Sam exploring this issue with him, and much to his credit, he was able to face how his interactions with Beth over the years were largely focused on what he wanted from her. He acknowledged having been selfish in his interactions with her and that he would complain when she did not give him what he wanted.

The three of us spent a lot of time trying to restore a healthier balance of giving and taking in the marriage. When one of them was too much in *take* mode, I would push them to think about giving more. Strangely, when one of them was too much in *give* mode, I would push them to think about receiving more, even if the other person complained about it for a while.

There are seasons in a marriage when the giving and the taking needs to be out of balance. For example, if a spouse is experiencing a serious medical issue, has lost a loved one, or is experiencing a psychological crisis, meeting their relational needs has to be front and center. When those seasons of life come into play, we need to be willing to focus on our spouse's needs and put our own on the back burner for the time being. In general, though, when we are not facing serious challenges like these, we need to make sure the giving and the taking is as equitable as possible.

The Three Kinds of Marital Takers

The view that Marlo Thomas expressed at the top of this chapter is that there are two kinds of people: givers and takers. Even though people are more complex and nuanced than that, let's go with it for now. Here I want to suggest that there are three kinds of *takers* in marriage. See if you fall into any of these categories.

The "Give to Get" Taker

One version of being a taker in marriage involves giving to your spouse in order to get what you want in return. For example, this kind of spouse might run an errand for you, but they want you to clean up the kitchen later that night in return. Here we are not really giving to our spouse, at least not in pure form. We give them something hoping to cash in later by them giving to us.

The "Quid Pro Quo" Taker

This kind of spouse is concerned about whether things in a marriage are equitable when it comes to giving and taking. They keep mental notes on who has given what to whom. When they are given more than they give, they feel anxious and guilt-ridden and that they need to catch back up. When they are giving more than they get, they feel bitter and resentful and that their spouse has to catch back up. Things are pretty much done quid pro quo—you scratch my back, and I'll scratch yours.

The "Full Blown" Taker

These are the spouses who are in marriage for what they can get out of it. These are the folks we accuse of being narcissistic, the "all about me" people. It is always about what they want from you, and while they might throw something your way on occasion, it is usually a breadcrumb compared to the seven-course meal you served them. The fact that the balance sheet of giving and taking is so out of whack is of no concern to them. In fact, they usually do not think it is out of whack because they feel they are giving to you by allowing you to be married to them. They take until you either have nothing left to give or become strong enough internally to stop being their supply source. Either way, they move on to the next poor soul they can use.

These are broad generalizations about how we human beings can be. Usually, we are a mixture of all these styles. In one relationship we might be more of a give-to-get person, in another we might lean toward being a quid pro quo giver-taker, and in another we might be a full-blown taker. The style of giving and taking we engage has a lot to do with the giving and taking style of the person we are with.

The "Give More Than You Take" Marriage

It is a no-brainer to say that marriage needs to be a place where we give more than we take. There is a huge risk in being a "give more than you take" kind of spouse in marriage, isn't there? What if we give a lot and our spouse doesn't return the favor? After a while, we can begin to feel like we are being exploited and allowing our spouse to treat us like a doormat.

Nevertheless, I would encourage you to go ahead and risk it. Someone has got to make the first move, so why not you? Risk giving more to your spouse than you receive and see how it changes the marriage. Maybe giving more to your spouse than they give to you will inspire them to return the favor. Even if it does not, you will have followed in the footsteps of Christ, who came to serve, not to be served (Matt. 20:28).

No marriage can afford to be an "I will give to you as long as you give to me" relationship. A godly marriage cannot be a 50–50 relationship. It has to be a 100–100 relationship, where both spouses are pouring themselves out as a drink offering to each other (2 Tim. 4:6). Do not lower the bar in your marriage and settle for anything less.

Not to belabor the point, but the attitude I want you to try to have in your marriage is: "What can I do to give to my spouse today? How can I meet their physical, emotional, and spiritual needs so they feel deeply loved and cherished? How can I put my needs on the back burner until I have made sure their needs are well taken care of? And how can I resist the urge to feel owed anything in return and trust that they love me and will be looking out for me as well?"

This is Christian love in a nutshell, dying on a daily basis to your selfishness, pouring yourself out like a drink offering, and going through each day seeking to serve and not be served. That is the way Christ lived his life, and he left a lot of people scratching their heads as a result. The world had never seen such a humble servant like him before, and it has not seen anyone like him since. Those are the footsteps we are supposed to follow, not only in our marriage but in all our relationships with others.

Not to speak out of the other side of my mouth, but I want to offer a quick thought about dealing with *abusive takers* in marriage. In this chapter, I am *not* encouraging you to give to your spouse in ways that would be unhealthy and lead to being treated abusively. For example, if your spouse says, "I want you to give me all the money you have so I can party every night," you need to draw firm boundaries with them about how money is going to be spent in the marriage. If your spouse were to say, "I want you to give me a three-hour back rub every night, but I'm not going to even hold your hand," you need to draw a firm boundary with them about the role of physical touch in the marriage. If your spouse were to say, "I want you to do all the chores around the house, but I'm not going to lift a finger to help you," you need to draw a firm boundary with them about shared responsibilities in the marriage. While we are to have a deep-seated spirit of giving more than we take in marriage, it is not to be a means by which a spouse is allowed to be exploitive and abusive.

So, when in doubt, give more than you take, but make sure you have healthy boundaries in place. Giving more than you take in marriage does not guarantee your spouse will return the favor, but at least you have set the bar at the proper biblical height, and it just might inspire your spouse to do the same.

Some Final Thoughts

Healthy giver, full-blown taker, or somewhere in between? To get along with our spouse, we need to keep moving in the direction of being a healthy giver: someone who desires to serve rather than be served, is discerning about when to give, is wise about how much to give, and allows others to give to them in return.

I want to challenge you in three important ways when it comes to giving and taking. First, honestly examine yourself as to whether you go into your marriage each day trying to serve your spouse or wanting them to serve you. Second, think through whether you are putting the proper boundaries around the giving and taking that occurs in your marriage so that no one is being taken advantage of. Third, take an honest look at whether you allow your spouse to give to you. Or are you so caught up in a toxic sense of shame that you stiff-arm your spouse when they want to serve you?

The issue of giving and taking in marriage requires a great deal of wisdom and discernment. Try not to lean on your own understanding in this area but seek God's wisdom when it comes to this matter in marriage. The devil is always in the extremes, so ask God to help you find the sweet spot of healthily giving to your spouse and allowing them to healthily give to you.

CHAPTER FIVE

Humble Yourself

An arrogant person considers himself perfect. This is the chief harm of arrogance. It interferes with a person's main task in life—becoming a better person.

—Leo Tolstoy

Do not think of yourself more highly than you ought, but rather think of yourself with sober judgment, in accordance with the faith that God has distributed to each of you.

—Romans 12:3

A Drug Enforcement Administration (DEA) officer stopped at a ranch in Texas to talk with an old rancher. He told the rancher, "I need to inspect your ranch for illegally growing drugs." The rancher said, "Okay, but don't go in that field over there—," as he pointed out the location.

The DEA officer verbally exploded, saying, "Mister, I have the authority of the federal government behind me!" Reaching into his rear pants pocket, the arrogant officer removed his badge and proudly displayed it to the rancher. "See this badge? This badge means I am allowed to go wherever I want . . . on any land! No questions asked or answers given! Have I made myself clear?"

The rancher nodded politely, apologized, and went about his chores. A short time later, the old rancher heard loud screams, looked up, and saw the DEA officer running for his life, being chased by the rancher's big Santa Gertrudis bull. With every step the bull was gaining ground on the officer, and it seemed likely that he'd sure enough get gored before he reached safety. The officer was clearly terrified. The rancher threw down his tools, ran to the fence, and yelled at the top of his lungs, "Your badge, show him your *badge*!"

Arrogant.

Not a pleasant word, is it? Few, if any, of us would like for that particular word to be the one that comes to mind when others think about us. Arrogant basically means that a person has an exaggerated sense of self-importance, an unrealistic feeling of superiority, and a sustained view of being better than others.

I think it is safe to say that most of us do not like being around arrogant people. How many times have we rolled our eyes to the back of our heads when we were around someone who talked about their talents, skills, intellect, and accomplishments in an over-the-top, "tons better than you" way? How many times have we found ourselves staying away from someone because he or she was way too full of themselves, would not honestly face the fact that they had flaws, and would not stop talking about themselves as if they were God's gift to the planet?

The arrogant, full-of-yourself person cannot get along well with others. None of us can stomp around the planet thinking we are superior to others and hope to pull off a healthy, loving bond with people. This is especially true in marriage. It is a major reason it is such a deadly mindset to have as we go through life.

When I work with couples, I am always on the prowl for where either spouse has an overly inflated view of themselves in their marriage. I am on the prowl for it because I know how damaging it can be to the couple getting along, much less thriving. Let me take you into my counseling office to drive this home.

The Husband Who Thought His Wife Was Lucky to Have Him

Sandra sat on my couch with the look of a woman too tired to keep going but too afraid to stop. She had been married to her husband, Nick, for twenty-five years, and they had two college-age girls. Sandra grew up in a working-class home and had to earn everything she got. Nick grew up in a wealthy family and pretty much had everything handed to him. Sandra grew up in a home where her mother and father constantly put her down, while Nick grew up in a home where his mother and father constantly told him how awesome and special he was.

The early years of Nick and Sandra's marriage were okay, but they were not especially close. Given Sandra's working-class background and overly critical parents, she always felt like a pair of brown shoes paired with a black tuxedo when around Nick's wealthy, prominent family. It did not help that she got the feeling Nick's parents looked down their nose at her and did not seem to think she was good enough for their son.

Sandra came to see me because she found out Nick had been having an affair with his best friend's wife, this after twenty-five years of marriage and two children. Though deeply hurt, she wanted to make the marriage work, but Nick had no interest in saving their relationship. As she looked back on their years together, Sandra could see Nick had always had one foot out the door from the very start of the marriage, and his affair was just the final straw.

"I can't sleep. I'm doing everything I can to let Nick know I forgive him and want him back, but he keeps telling me it's over," Sandra says, with tears streaming down her face.

"He's not willing even to consider working on the marriage?" I ask.

"Well, he says he is, but if actions speak louder than words, I don't think so."

"What actions are you referring to?"

"He said he needed some space, so he moved out and got his own apartment. I think it was just an excuse to be with her."

"What else?"

"He won't go to church with me; he doesn't interact with me except about things related to our kids and finances."

"What else?"

"Well, I feel like the biggest fool to say this, but he won't cut the relationship off with this woman."

"He what?"

"He won't stop seeing this woman. She's planning on divorcing her husband and wants to spend the rest of her life with him. He hasn't made a commitment to her yet, but he's sure setting his life up to do just that."

"What kinds of things has he said to you in the midst of all this?"

"That he never wanted to marry me. That he did it out of fear he wouldn't find anyone better. That he always looked down on me given my family background. That he wasn't proud to have me for a wife. And the cruelest blow of all, that I was lucky to have him all these years."

"He said what?"

"That I was lucky to have him."

"How have you been dealing with all this?"

"I have too many glasses of wine in the evening, consume sweets like there's no tomorrow, spend money like it's going out of style, watch tons of sad movies on TV . . . and I came to see you."

"Well, I'm glad you did."

"I appreciate it. This has turned my world upside down, and Nick doesn't care. He's as cold as ice to me these days. He actually seems to be . . . happy . . . to be with this woman and excited about their future life together. Our kids are devastated and trying to talk some sense into him, but he has turned a deaf ear to all of us."

"Sandra, I'm so sorry. I know this is killing you inside. We'll roll up our sleeves together to help you get through it and come out on the other side better off."

My heart broke for Sandra. She had spent the past twenty-five years of her life getting the message from Nick and his family that she was not good enough for him. That message only fed the internal narrative of her life—she was not good enough for anyone and unworthy of being loved by others. Sandra could not bring herself to divorce Nick even though he continued to throw his relationship with the other woman in her face. He ultimately divorced her and went off to build a new life with the other woman.

Sandra's situation broke my heart. Nick's unbridled arrogance toward her led him to move on to what he thought were greener pastures with another woman. As further proof that pride goes before the fall, Nick's relationship with this other woman did not work out, and he lost everything in the process—his wife, two children, job, and standing in the community, an incredibly high price for what turned out to be an adulterous fling.

Pride goes before a fall. It certainly did in Nick's case, and it came at the expense of his wife and children. The enemy wants us to think more highly of ourselves than we ought because he knows it leads to all kinds of destructive acting out, sometimes at the expense of a marriage and a family.

Three Kinds of Arrogance in Marriage

There are three basic kinds of arrogance in marriage that hinder our ability to get along with our spouse. Which version, if any, do you struggle with?

Thinking Too Highly of Yourself

This is what we typically associate with someone being arrogant—they have a higher view of themselves than is warranted by who they really are. Their view of who they are greatly exceeds the reality of their actual self.

When we think we are far better than we really are, we are out of touch with reality and going to interact with others in a condescending and dismissive way. This was how Nick viewed himself in his marriage to Sandra before it came crashing to an end. He thought he was better than Sandra and acted on that erroneous belief by committing adultery with another man's wife.

Thinking Too Lowly of Yourself

Strangely enough, we are being inversely arrogant when we think more negatively about ourselves than what is accurate. This takes the form of thinking we are worthless and unworthy of love and minimizing our strengths, talents, and abilities. It is just as out of touch with reality as someone thinking they are awesome and better than everyone else.

This was the struggle Sandra had in how she viewed herself in her marriage to Nick. She thought so poorly of herself that she allowed Nick to keep telling her she was beneath him, throwing his affair in her face, and publicly humiliating her. She could not bring herself to divorce him and kept clinging to the idea that Nick would turn around and become a humble, loving husband who was good for her.

Mixed Arrogance

These individuals, perhaps the largest group, bounce back and forth between "I'm awesome and entitled to love" and "I'm awful and unworthy of love." They are split between these two extremes when it comes to how they view themselves. Sometimes they feel entitled to love and are dismissive of others who do not worship the ground they walk on. Sometimes they feel unworthy of love and allow themselves to be treated in a denigrating manner. It can be a little harder to interact with this kind of person because you never know which state they are in, something that can be crazy-making in the relationship.

No form of arrogance is a good thing, and we need to do whatever we can to reject these false views of ourselves. Doing so is what the Bible refers to as having humility. Properly understood, humility is the willingness to see yourself *accurately*—your strengths and weaknesses, good qualities and bad. If we can keep working on an accurate sense of self, we can avoid the extremes of thinking either too highly or too lowly of ourselves and interact with others in a sane and loving manner.

The "Humble Yourself" Marriage

We cannot afford to enter our marriage each day thinking we are far better or far worse than our spouse given that neither is true. Sure, we may have some strengths our spouse does not have, but our spouse has some strengths we do not have. The flip side is true as well. We have weaknesses and liabilities our spouse does not have, and they have weaknesses and liabilities we do not have. In the grand scheme of things, though, we are not significantly better or worse than our spouse in our overall spiritual, psychological, and moral health, at least not compared to Jesus Christ.

In far too many marriages, spouses can tend to look down their nose at each other and have a superiority complex when it comes to how they compare themselves to their mate. Some people have the opposite, an inferiority complex that leads them to think they are so much less than their spouse. Sadly, in this day and age, it is more common for people to think they are better than their spouse and walk around all high and mighty in marriage.

With few exceptions, the person you married is "just right" for you given your overall level of spiritual and psychological health. A spirit of humility about that goes a long way in marriage. If I could make you think correctly about this matter, I would program into your mind the following belief: "In the grand scheme of things, I am no better or worse than the person I married. We each have our strengths, and we each have our weaknesses. Together, we will humbly encourage each other to hold on to what is good about ourselves and let go of what is bad. We will affirm each other's positive qualities and humbly challenge each other's negative qualities as we go through life together. With God's help, we will live each and every day as equals and fight the good fight of living life together the best way we know how."

Here are some tips on how to humble yourself in marriage so you can get along better with your spouse.

First, humbling yourself means seeing your strengths, abilities, talents, and competencies as they really are. It means calling a spade a spade when it comes to acknowledging the good, positive things you bring to the table each day. Humbling yourself means you own the fact that the good things about you leave your marriage and the world better off when properly expressed.

Second, humbling yourself means seeing your flaws, defects, and weaknesses as they really are. You call a spade a spade here as well in terms of acknowledging the reality that there is a dark, defective side to who you are, and you acknowledge that when you act out of your fallen self, you harm yourself, your spouse, and the world you live in.

Third, humbling yourself leads to courageously holding on to the things about you that are good and changing the things about you that are bad. You remain true to the positive qualities and traits God put in you and make sure they grow and develop over time. You let go of the negative qualities and traits you have fallen into along the way and make sure they atrophy over time.

Finally, humbling yourself means you do not look down your nose at others nor walk around hanging your head. The more you acknowledge your strengths and weaknesses, the more you see yourself as a human being who is just like everyone else. Humbling yourself leads you to feel more like a member of the human race, not less of one. You stop seeing people as "alien" or "other," and you start seeing how, in all the ways that truly matter, we are similar to each other.

Humbling yourself is especially important in marriage. Honestly acknowledging your good and bad qualities helps keep it real between you and your spouse and gives the two of you a chance to have healthy, reality-based interactions with each other. Courageously holding on to your good qualities and letting go of your bad ones helps strengthen the quality of your interactions over time. Finally, it leads to seeing your spouse as similar, not different, someone you can identify with rather than misunderstand.

Some Final Thoughts

I was taught growing up that being humble meant you were down on yourself. The other side of this was being taught you were arrogant if you thought there was anything about you that was good or worthwhile. In a religious context, it was called "worm theology," as in, "Oh, what a wretched worm am I!"

I don't see things that way anymore, and I do not want you to, either. We are all fallen and have a dark side, and that aspect of who we are is certainly wretched. At the same time, we are fearfully and wonderfully made in the image of God and capable of acting in ways that are kind, compassionate, and loving.

In marriage, it can be hard to walk the fine line between having a deeply fallen side to who we are while acknowledging and living into being made by God in his image. However hard that line is to walk, though, I want you to walk it in your marriage. Enter your marriage each day humbly aware of just how flawed and fallen you are, while staying aware of having been created by the God of the universe with wonderful attributes and qualities that reflect who he is.

The challenge in every Christian marriage is to walk according to the Spirit and not the flesh (Gal. 5:16). This is easier said than done, but that is why we need to turn to God's power for help to do it. Humility is the key attribute here. Without it, we cannot interact with our spouse in a loving, growth-promoting way. Without it, we will think either too highly or too lowly of ourselves and our spouse and be unable to thrive in marriage.

In your day-to-day interactions with your spouse, I want you to work as hard as you can to let God help you see yourself and your partner accurately. I want you to let God help you see all the wonderful qualities, talents, and abilities he put in both of you, and I want you to let him help you see the things both of you have become that he never intended you to be. Do not shrink back from either. To do so is to fall back into the arrogance of thinking too highly or too lowly of yourself, and you will make it harder for your marriage to thrive.

I close with one of my favorite quotes on humility, this one from theologian Thomas Merton:

> It is almost impossible to overestimate the value of true humility and its power in the spiritual life. For the beginning of humility is the beginning of blessedness and the consummation of humility is the perfection of all joy. Humility contains in itself the answer to all the great problems of the life of the soul. It is the only key to faith, with which the spiritual life begins: for faith and humility are inseparable. In perfect humility all selfishness disappears and your soul no longer lives for itself or in itself for God: and it is lost and submerged in Him and transformed into Him.[1]

Let's strive to be as humble as possible in marriage. Let's not think more highly or lowly of ourselves or our spouse than we ought. Let's strive to be as accurate in our view of ourselves and our spouse as possible so that our interactions with each other are characterized by empathy, compassion, and kindness. Let's remember that we are all fearfully and wonderfully made image bearers desperately in need of a Savior.

---

[1] Thomas Merton, *New Seeds of Contemplation* (New Directions, 2007), 181.

CHAPTER SIX

Get Your Mind Right

The mind is its own place, and in itself can make
a Heaven of Hell, a Hell of Heaven.

—John Milton

Do not conform to the pattern of this world, but be
transformed by the renewing of your mind.

—Romans 12:2

A young man named John received a parrot as a gift. The problem was, the parrot had a bad attitude and an even worse vocabulary. Every word out of the bird's mouth was rude, obnoxious, and laced with profanity. John tried and tried to change the bird's attitude by consistently saying only polite words, playing soft music, and doing anything else he could think of to "clean up" the bird's vocabulary, but to no avail.

Finally, John was fed up and he yelled at the parrot. The parrot yelled back. John shook the parrot, and the parrot got angrier and even more rude. In desperation, John threw up his hands, grabbed the bird and put him in the freezer. For a few minutes the parrot squawked and kicked and screamed. Then suddenly there was total quiet. Not a peep was heard for over a minute. Fearing that he had killed the parrot, John quickly opened the door to the freezer. The parrot calmly stepped out onto John's outstretched arms and said, "I believe I may have offended you with my rude language and actions. I am sincerely remorseful for my inappropriate transgressions, and I fully intend to do everything I can to correct my rude and unforgivable behavior."

John was stunned at the change in the bird's attitude. As he was about to ask the parrot what had made such a dramatic change in his behavior, the bird continued, "May I ask what the chicken did?"

No relationship can rise above the mindset people carry into it. If your mindset is accurate, clear, and rational, you are likely to get along pretty well with others. If your mindset is inaccurate, distorted, and irrational, the chances of you getting along with others are slim and none. Your beliefs, attitudes, and expectations govern the quality of your relationships and can help you soar to new heights or sink to new lows in your interactions with people. Unfortunately, all of us have faulty ways of viewing others that lead to disharmony and conflict in relationships. To put it differently, we do not have our heads screwed on straight when it comes to how we think about people, ourselves included. This is especially true in marriage. None of us enter marriage with our minds right when it comes to the thoughts we carry into this most important of all relationships.

Our faulty beliefs and attitudes damage our ability to get close to our spouse. They put a low ceiling over how connected and attached we can be with the person we married. There are literally dozens of foul-smelling beliefs and attitudes we fall into in marriage, too many to go into in this chapter. I'm going to zero in on one especially odorous attitude in marriage. Let me forewarn you, you suffer from this attitude more than you realize, and so does your spouse.

An Entitled Couple

Allen and Mary Beth were newly married, but they were already experiencing a fair amount of conflict in their marriage. They loved each other and were perplexed as to how something so good could go so bad so quickly. They came to me for help to figure out why.

"Dr. Thurman, we fight like cats and dogs. We weren't this way when we dated, but we sure are this way now," Mary Beth starts the conversation.

"Yeah, we just can't seem to get along no matter what we do. Everything becomes a fight, and we never resolve anything," Allen adds.

"Give me an example of one of your recent fights," I suggest.

"Well, just the other day, we got into a fight about who should get the garbage can to the curb for trash pickup. I thought Allen should do it, and he thought I should do it," Mary Beth says.

"Any idea why the two of you thought the other should do it?" I ask.

"Well, on my end, I do the dishes every night, so I thought Allen should get the garbage to the curb," Mary Beth says.

"And, on my end, I do the laundry every night, and I thought Mary Beth should get the garbage down to the curb," Allen adds.

"I may be jumping in here too quickly, but I think I see what your problem is," I suggest.

"What is it?" Mary Beth asks.

"Yeah, what is it?" Allen asks.

"I think both of you have an entitlement problem," I offer.

"A what?" Allen asks.

"An entitlement problem," I respond.

"I'm not tracking with you . . . can you say more?" Mary Beth responds.

"Sure. It seems to me that both of you look at what you do around the house and feel it entitles you to the other doing their part. Mary Beth, you do the dishes every night, so you feel entitled to Allen getting the garbage to the curb. Allen, you do the laundry every night, so you feel entitled to Mary Beth taking the garbage to the curb," I reply.

"Isn't that reasonable?" Allen asks.

"No, not really. I know it sounds like I'm telling you one plus one equals a bucket of kumquats, but each of you doing the things you do in the marriage doesn't entitle you to your spouse doing what you want them to do," I suggest, knowing that my brilliance and wisdom as a marriage therapist will not go over too well.

"It doesn't? How can any couple get along if they can't expect the other to do their fair share?" Mary Beth asks.

"Well, you just mentioned the key word . . . expect. Whenever we *expect* a spouse to do something, we're actually saying we feel entitled to them doing it . . . that they owe it to us," I reply.

"They don't?" Allen asks.

"No, they don't. When Mary Beth does the dishes, that doesn't entitle her to you getting the garbage down to the curb. When you do the laundry, that doesn't entitle you to Mary Beth getting the garbage down to the curb. If it's any comfort to you, this is a common mindset in marriage, but it is deadly to marital harmony," I answer.

"Why? Why is it so harmful to how we get along?" Mary Beth asks.

"Well, one of the main reasons it's harmful is that when your spouse actually does what you expect them to do, you don't really appreciate it. Why? Because, in your head, they're just doing what they should do, what you expected them to do. Your lack of gratitude about what they did is disrespectful, and your spouse isn't going to like it," I add.

"So, if I hear you right, we're fighting like cats and dogs because we feel entitled to each other doing what we want them to do, is that right?" Allen says.

"Yes, that's right. Without realizing it, you have a spirit of entitlement in your marriage, and it's killing your appreciation and enjoyment of each other," I reply.

"Man, that's not good," Allen says.

"No, that's not good," Mary Beth agrees.

"So, what do we do about it?" Allen asks.

"Well, we're going to work on a lot of things in here, but one thing I'm going to push you to do is switch from an attitude of entitlement to a humbler attitude of 'I would appreciate it if . . .'" I suggest.

"What do you mean?" Mary Beth asks.

"Well, let's go back to the issue of getting the garbage can down to the curb. Let me suggest that regardless of how much or little you did that day to contribute to the functioning of the marriage, you simply say, 'Sweetheart, would you mind getting the garbage down to the curb?' with no whiff of expecting it or feeling entitled to it."

"So, there's a big difference between feeling entitled to things from your spouse and wanting or desiring things from your spouse. Is that right?" Mary Beth asks.

"Spot on . . . you should have become a psychologist," I playfully respond.

All of us walk around with a spirit of entitlement in marriage, and it generates a lot of bitterness and resentment when our spouse does not do what we expect. Even when they do what we expect them to do, we do not really appreciate it. An entitlement attitude is especially destructive in marriage given that one of our most important psychological needs is appreciation. If neither spouse expresses much appreciation for what their partner does each day, it is incredibly discouraging and often leads to one or both spouses no longer doing anything to help the common good.

I was able to help Mary Beth and Allen overcome their sense of entitlement in the marriage and change it out for a humble spirit of "Would you be willing to?" For them, it made all the difference. But I was only able to help them because they were willing to let me. They were humble enough to see that an attitude of entitlement was prideful and arrogant and going to continue to damage their marriage.

Not every couple is willing to join me in overcoming a spirit of entitlement. Some couples are rigidly bought into a quid pro quo mindset in marriage and really do feel entitled to their spouse meeting their demands and expectations. Some destructive attitudes die hard, and only couples who dedicate themselves to renewing their minds in marriage make much progress.

It is always a wonderful thing when a couple comes to grips with the faulty beliefs and attitudes they bring into their marriage. They grow in their appreciation that when it comes to the human mind, "garbage in, garbage out." The more willing we are to atrophy the faulty tapes and strengthen the good ones that play in our mind each day, the healthier and more loving our marriages become.

The Lies Couples Believe

The issue of faulty thinking has been an area of special interest for me throughout my career as a psychologist. In this section, I want to walk you through a book I wrote, *The Lies Couples Believe*, to give you a better feel for the kinds of erroneous beliefs and attitudes that can sink a marriage.

We bring a wide variety of misguided beliefs into marriage, too numerous to count. Here I want to briefly mention the ten I cover in my book. Here goes.

The Purpose of Marriage Is to Make Me Happy

The main purpose of marriage is to help us grow into full-fledged, loving adults, not make us happy. While it is understandable we want to be happy in marriage, we need to raise the bar higher than that and allow God to use our marriages to help us mature into healthier, more mature people. If we allow God to use our marriages to help us mature, we will end up being about as happy in marriage as we could hope to be.

My Spouse Can Completely Meet All My Needs

Our spouse cannot meet all our needs. No one can. That is why God works through a variety of resources to "meet all your needs according to the riches of his glory in Christ Jesus" (Phil. 4:19). We need to avoid the expectation that our spouse can meet all of our emotional needs. It is too much for any one person to tackle, and it leaves both spouses feeling frustrated, inadequate, and discouraged.

My Spouse Is a Bigger Mess of a Human Being Than I Am

We are just as big of a mess as our spouse. While we may be messes in different ways, we are not better than our spouse spiritually, psychologically, or morally, at least not to the degree that we have anything to crow about. If we want to stay humble about this, we need to compare ourselves to Jesus Christ each day. If we do that, we will never look down our nose at our spouse.

I Am Entitled to My Spouse's Love

We covered this earlier, but entitlement is a narcissistic attitude we bring into marriage, and it gets in the way of having a loving, respectful, and appreciative closeness with our spouse. Every day of marriage, we need to drop our spirit of entitlement at the door and humbly desire to be loved by our spouse, not expect it or demand it.

Our Marital Problems Are All My Spouse's Fault

The vast majority of problems in marriage are co-created, and each person needs to take full responsibility for their unhealthy contribution to why the marriage is not going well. Marriage is a "takes two to tango" relationship, and both spouses are culpable for the problems they have. Even if a spouse is the main reason for a *particular* problem in the marriage, how we respond can become just as big of a problem.

My Spouse Should Accept Me Just the Way I Am

We need to accept our spouse "warts and all," all their good, the bad, and the ugly. That being said, accepting each other warts and all is not to be interpreted as your spouse liking everything about you or not ever wanting you to change. I do not mean to hurt anyone's feelings here, but not everything about us is likeable. In fact, some things about us are highly unlikeable and need to change. So, yes, we need to accept each other warts and all, but we need to have firm boundaries with each other in marriage about the especially bad warts we have and challenge each other to remove them.

My Spouse Should Be Just Like Me

If we are in our right mind, we do not want to be married to our clone. Variety is the spice of life, and it is a good thing we are different from our spouse because it leads to "iron sharpens iron" (Prov. 27:17) growth in marriage. Plus, given that we all have flaws and defects, we certainly don't want our spouse to be like us in those ways. Sure, we want our spouse to be like us in the positive traits we possess, but we do not want our spouse to be like us when it comes to our bad qualities.

I See My Spouse for Who They Really Are

We all have an inaccurate view of our spouse, one that keeps us from seeing them for who they truly are. We all "look through a glass darkly" when it comes to how we see our spouse. Typically, we do not give them enough credit for their positive qualities and too much negative credit for their bad ones. All of us have a distorted view of the person we are married to, and a big part of getting along better in marriage is to ask God to help us see our spouse the way he does—accurately.

My Spouse Has to Earn My Forgiveness

We will explore this more deeply in an upcoming chapter, but forgiveness is not something our spouse should ever have to earn. We are *commanded* by God to forgive a person when they mistreat us (Eph. 4:32). When our spouse wounds us, we need to make sure we do not attach any conditions to forgiving them for what they did.

We Can Reconcile without Repenting

Two things are required for a couple to reconcile when there has been a rupture in the relationship. First, the *offending* spouse has to be *genuinely sorry* for what they did, ask for forgiveness, and repentantly move in a better direction. Second, the *offended* spouse has to be willing to forgive. If either spouse refuses to do their part, reconciliation is not possible. Far too often, couples sweep relationship ruptures under the carpet, thinking they have done what it takes to reconcile, only to find out later on that the rupture was never properly repaired.

This is just a small sampling of the numerous unbiblical beliefs and attitudes couples bring into marriage. Because of the phenomena of "garbage in, garbage out," every marital relationship is damaged by these erroneous ways of thinking. This is why one of the main themes in the Bible is, "Be transformed by the renewing of your mind" (Rom. 12:2).

For our marriages to heal and become tender and loving, we have to turn to God for help to overcome our faulty beliefs by deeply internalizing beliefs that are true, noble, lovely, pure, and worthwhile (Phil. 4:8). This is always hard work, but it is always worth it given the wonderful relationship results that are waiting on us.

The "Get Your Mind Right" Marriage

Here let's focus on changing the faulty view of entitlement to get your mind right in marriage. I will leave it up to the lesson in the workbook on this topic to help you make further progress in this area. You are doing the workbook, aren't you?

When I speak publicly on the topic of entitlement in marriage, I can sometimes hear the audience mutter, if not actually grumble. I like to rattle people's cages when I give a talk, so I usually go into this topic by saying something outlandish like, "You are not entitled to your spouse's love, kindness, faithfulness, support, attention, affection, understanding, or anything else you think you are entitled to in marriage." I am sure you can understand why people in the audience might mutter and grumble at that point in my talk and why a lively discussion ensues.

Here is the deal when it comes to marriage: You are not entitled to anything. Like it or not, getting married does not entitle you to your spouse's love and the fifty other things you think it entitles you to.

Now you might be tempted to say, "But, Doc, don't we make a vow to love each other until death do us part? Doesn't that vow entitle me to my spouse's love?" Yes, we do vow to love each other through thick and thin, but making a vow is simply a way of saying, "Marriage is so blasted hard that we need to vow our love to each other, otherwise we would leave the minute things get tough." Making a vow to stay together is just the two of you acknowledging that marriage requires a strong commitment at its core, and it is not a hall pass from God to feel entitled to your spouse loving you.

Let me drive this home with some examples from my own marriage. If I work hard all day, does that entitle me to Holly working hard all day, too? If I am kind to Holly, does that entitle me to her being kind to me in return? If I don't steal her favorite snack from the pantry, does that entitle me to her leaving my favorite snack alone? If I do her laundry for her, does that entitle me to her doing my laundry for me? I would argue that across the board the answer is a categorical no. *Nothing we do or are entitles us to our spouse doing or being those things in return.*

So if you are not entitled to anything from your spouse, how should you think about marriage? I encourage you to work on your entitlement issues by making the mental shift from "I'm entitled to . . . from my spouse" to "I want . . . from my spouse." That one attitudinal shift in marriage can make all the difference.

If you go from "I'm entitled to my spouse being kind to me" to "I want my spouse to be kind to me," you are on the way to breaking free from all the resentment and bitterness entitlement leads to when it goes unfulfilled. Unfulfilled *entitlement* demands and expectations lead to resentment and bitterness and a mean-spirited reaction toward your spouse when they do not deliver the goods. On the other side of the coin, unfulfilled *wants* simply lead to disappointment and an appropriate sense of hurt, sadness, and frustration. Trade all your resentment and bitterness in for feeling sad, disappointed, and hurt when your spouse does not give you what you want. It is an important trade-off to make each day.

Some Final Thoughts

I honestly believe thoughts have a smell to them. Our true, lovely, pure, and excellent thoughts smell like Chanel No. 5, and they can fill a marriage relationship with a wonderful aroma. Our untrue, ugly, impure, and non-excellent thoughts smell like . . . well, I think you get the point . . . and can fill our marital relationship with a foul stench. This is why when your spouse enters a room, you can smell whether they have a good or a bad attitude and why you are either drawn toward them or want to spend the rest of the evening in a different room (if not a different time zone!).

This helps explain why we psychologists say people suffer from "stinking thinking." Because our heads are not screwed on straight and our "thinkers" are broken, we have a lot of smelly thoughts each day. Those foul-smelling thoughts generate foul-smelling emotions and actions in how we react to our spouse mistreating us. Whatever else it takes to have a great marriage, it takes getting our minds right.

I encourage you to keep working on getting your mind right in marriage. If you work hard enough at it, you can go from a mind full of falsehoods and misbeliefs to a mind full of what is true, lovely, pure, and worthwhile. You can go from "garbage in, garbage out" to "good stuff in, good stuff out." You can go from a mind full of foul-smelling thoughts to a mind full of pleasant-smelling ones. The truth really can set you free to love your spouse in a deeper and healthier way than you ever thought possible.

CHAPTER SEVEN

Stop Talking Trash

I don't talk trash; I talk smack. They're totally different. Trash talk is all hypothetical, like, "Your momma's so fat, she could eat the Internet." But smack talk is happening, like, right now. Like, "You're ugly and I know it for a fact 'cause I got the evidence right there."

—Kelly Kapoor, *The Office*

Do not let any unwholesome talk come out of your mouths, but only what is helpful for building others up according to their needs, that it may benefit those who listen.

—Ephesians 4:29

A guy got up to give his best man speech at a wedding. Here is what he said.

"I'm really happy for Rob and Sarah. It's great that Sarah can start this new chapter in her life, in her relationship. So, this is for all of you guys out there—she is off the market. She's not that type of girl anymore. We know she has somewhat of a past, but she's not that type of girl anymore. So, you really have to understand this, no more calling or texting her. This is a new chapter in her life. No more visiting her apartment or late-night rendezvous. You gotta just leave her alone now. So, I'm going to have to ask everyone to bring up their keys to her apartment."

After saying that, he put out a bowl for people to drop their keys in. Everyone started filing up and putting keys in the bowl, with a little old man being the final person to do so.

Unbeknownst to Rob and Sarah, the best man had handed out keys to all the guys prior to the reception and totally fabricated everything he said about Sarah. This is the kind of inappropriate thing best men sometimes do at weddings, and it would have been more than understandable if both Rob and Sarah were a little miffed about it. It would have been especially understandable if Sarah were upset about what the best man did given that she was the focus of his not-so-funny actions.

My wife Holly loves Jane Austen. When she is going to binge-watch movies or television shows, she hunkers down with *Sense and Sensibility*, *Pride and Prejudice*, *Emma*, *Persuasion*, *Northanger Abbey*, and *Mansfield Park*. On occasion, when I weaken as a man, she talks me into watching these shows with her. I hate to admit it, but I like them, too. Please do not tell anyone; I have a reputation to protect.

One thing that strikes me when I watch these shows is how respectfully and civilly people talked to each other back then. It is impressive how carefully they chose their words and how civil and articulate they were when expressing their thoughts and feelings, even when they were hurt or angry about something.

Jump to the twenty-first century, and you do not hear people talk to each other the way they used to in Jane Austen's time. No, it is a fundamentally different day and age when it comes to how people converse with each other, especially when they are hacked off. Our modern conversations do not come anywhere close to reaching the high bar of that period of verbal civility. Our exchanges with each other are often filled with hateful, foul, and denigrating words meant to tear someone down, not build them up.

To get along with our spouse, we have to change our conversational style. We have to stop using words that wound and start using words that heal. We have to turn away from words that denigrate and lean in to words that edify. In more updated lingo, we need to avoid talking trash to our spouse. The Free Dictionary defines talking trash as making "disparaging, insulting, or abusive comments" about someone.[2] We need to avoid doing this at all costs in marriage.

Getting along well with our spouse and talking trash are mutually exclusive. We simply cannot talk to our spouse in a verbally abusive manner and end up with anything but a damaged relationship that will be hard to repair. If we do not radically raise the level of verbal civility in our marriages, we are going to have a hard time getting along in a loving and connected manner.

Let me take you into my counseling office to drive this home.

The Trash-Talking Twins

Evan and Lilly had been married for ten years when they came to see me. They had two small children under the age of five. They met on a dating site after a string of unsuccessful relationships. During a turbulent time of getting to know each other, they often got into it with each other in terms of talking harshly and abusively.

After they got married, things got worse. Both ratcheted up the abusiveness of how they said things to each other and also increased the abusiveness of the words they would use. That led to them dropping themselves into my office for some help.

"I just can't stand the way Evan talks to me, Dr. Thurman. He is so incredibly condescending and dismissive all the time," Lilly opens the session.

"Well, that's interesting," Evan fires back. "You're the most disrespectful person I know. No one else talks to me the way you do!"

"See, that's what I'm talking about! He constantly dismisses what I say about him and turns everything back on me," she responds.

"I do not. I just don't agree with what you're saying. Do you want me to be some kind of stooge who agrees with everything you say?" he replies.

"How about you listen to what I say before you disagree with it? Is that too much to ask, you jerk?" Lilly shoots back with a condescending tone.

"Well, there you go again. You're condescending toward me when you think I'm being condescending to you. Why don't you quit being such a

---

[2] *Farlex Dictionary of Idioms*, s.v. "talking trash," accessed November 25, 2024, https://idioms.thefreedictionary.com/talking+trash.

hypocrite and start practicing what you preach?" Evan answers, putting Lilly down in the process.

"I will if you will," she replies.

"Oh, how mature! You'll start talking nicer to me if I start talking nicer to you? Are you a child? Why can't you just be mature enough to talk to me respectfully no matter how I talk to you?" Evan asks, unaware of how hypocritical his request is.

"So, I'm just supposed to sit here and take all your verbal abuse and respond like a mature adult?" Lilly almost shouts.

"Yeah, try it, you might like it," Evan responds sarcastically.

"You can forget it. Don't ask me to do anything you're not willing to do. Talk about being a hypocrite!" she answers.

"Let me jump in if that's okay?" I ask.

"Please do," Lilly replies.

"We're not paying you for nothing," Evan says, being passive-aggressive toward me.

"It pains me to see the two of you interact this way, and I know it's painful for you as well. I know you love each other, but the way you talk to each other is unloving, even abusive. One of the main reasons you don't get along is that neither of you is willing to talk to the other in a civil and respectful manner. You're in a standoff with each other, waiting for the other one to talk nicely to you before returning the favor. How's that so far?" I ask.

"Spot on," Evan replies.

"Yes, that's right," Lilly agrees.

"So, I have a question for you. Are you willing to raise the bar much higher for how you talk to each other and stop the trash talking?" I ask.

"I will if she will," Evan replies.

"Evan, that won't work. Both of you need to make a commitment to stop being verbally abusive whether the other person agrees to it or not. If both of you don't go all-in on this, you're going to go back to the same destructive place every time you interact," I respond, standing my ground.

"I'm not sure I'm there yet," he answers, being honest about his struggle to take the higher road and treat Lilly properly, whether she treats him that way or not.

"I appreciate your honesty, Evan, but this is not negotiable. Let me be honest with both of you. Your relationship is actually my client, not the two of you. I have an obligation to look out for and protect your relationship, and that is going to mean calling both of you out when you do anything that damages it. Being verbally abusive to each other is damaging your marriage, and I wouldn't be doing my job if I didn't demand that you stop. Do you understand what I'm saying?" I ask.

"Yes, I get it," Evan responds.

"I do, too," Lilly answers.

"Okay, so here are your marching orders for today. I want you to go home and talk this over. I want you to talk about how corrosive the way you talk to each other has been over the years. I want you to be honest with each other about whether you're willing to work with me to do something about it. If both of you are willing to work on this, I'm happy to be your counselor. If one or both of you are not, I will refer you elsewhere. Are we on the same page about this?" I reply.

"Yes."

"Yes."

I am happy to report Evan and Lilly humbled themselves about the destructive role of verbal abuse in their marriage. Both of them made a courageous commitment to face how verbally and emotionally abusive they were to each other and do something constructive about it. They were able to come under genuine conviction that how they talked to each other was unacceptable and had to stop.

It was not always smooth sailing with Evan and Lilly. Their habit of being verbally abusive was deeply ingrained in how they talked to each other. Nevertheless, we weathered the setbacks and stayed the course toward raising the communication bar in their marriage. As we did, greater warmth and tenderness toward each other began to grow, they managed conflict in a more respectful manner, and they became more loving toward each other. The icing on the cake is that they began to model for their children how mature adults are supposed to talk to each other so their children might have a brighter interpersonal future.

The Most Damaging Kinds of Trash Talking in Marriage

I want to take you into fourteen different categories of verbal abuse the experts in this area have identified. These different forms of verbal abuse overlap with each other to some degree, but they are distinct enough to warrant their own category. It goes without saying that if we fall into any of these types of verbal abuse in how we talk to our spouse, we are not going to get along with them very well, and they probably will not want to be around us.

Discounting

Denying that your spouse has a right to their thoughts or feelings. It's telling them they are being too sensitive, emotional, or childish. For example, "You're overreacting to what I did and need to chill out."

Biting Humor

Using humor to put your spouse down. For example, "That meal you made tonight is going to set culinary arts back for decades."

Blaming

Holding your spouse responsible for things that are outside their control or sphere of influence. For example, "It's your fault you didn't get the job you applied for," when there were hundreds of applicants, many of whom were more qualified.

Judging

Negatively evaluating your spouse and putting them down in the process. For example, "You don't help me enough around the house because you're lazy and selfish."

Trivializing

Making what your spouse wants or does seem small and insignificant. For example, "You wanting to be on the school board isn't that big of a deal, so stop worrying about it!"

Threatening

Making explicit threats about what you are going to do if your spouse does not do what you want. For example, "I'm going to divorce you and take the kids if you don't start treating me better."

Name-Calling

Calling your spouse derogatory names. For example, "You're such a loser—nothing you do ever turns out well."

Denying and Rationalizing

Refusing to acknowledge your bad behavior or attempting to justify it. For example, "I don't have a drinking problem, and if I do, it's because I'm under so much pressure at work."

Being Tonal

Using the tone of your voice to put your spouse down. For example, sarcastically saying, "You really did a great job cleaning the house today—thanks so much," when they did not clean the house at all.

Manipulating

Using words to manipulate your spouse into giving you what you want. For example, "If you really loved me, you would take me on a cruise for our anniversary."

Not Taking Responsibility

Not owning your feelings or actions but instead blaming them on your spouse. For example, "It's your fault I got mad and stormed out of the restaurant because you were being rude to me!"

Making Accusations

Repetitively accusing your spouse of something because of your own insecurities or arrogance. For example, "You don't really love me, do you?" or "You don't love me as much as I love you."

Being Bossy

Frequently telling your spouse what to do. For example, "Get me a water bottle from the kitchen," or "Take my clothes to the laundry."

Being Condescending

Looking down your nose at your spouse because you think you are better than them. For example, "You need to become more organized like me. Maybe then you will be as productive as I am."

From the length of this list, you do not need me to tell you that there are a lot of different ways to talk trash to your spouse and for them to talk trash to you. If we are not careful, we can fall into any one of these ways of being verbally abusive to our spouse, and, at times, our spouse may have talked to us this way as well. When we default to talking trash to our spouse like this (or them trash-talking us), the marriage is going to take a big hit, and we are not going to get along very well with each other.

The "Stop Talking Trash" Marriage

I wish I could adequately convey to you how important it is to stop talking trash to your spouse. We say in my line of work that "words are like punches," and if I had my way, we would all equate verbal abuse to physically punching our spouse. If we could see it that way, we might be tempted to turn ourselves in to the police for assault and battery, given all the wounding things we sometimes say.

While none of the ways of being verbally abusive we explored are acceptable, I want to briefly zero in on three that are especially deadly in marriage: criticizing, trivializing, and rationalizing. These three leave a devastating mark on a spouse's soul, and unless you stop doing them, your partner cannot heal, and the two of you cannot properly repair the ruptures that occur in your relationship.

Criticizing your spouse is always out of line, yet we do it a lot in marriage. Some of us are supercritical individuals who can leave our spouse wondering if they ever do anything right. When we are coming from a perfectionistic point of view, our spouse *cannot* do anything right because as a human being, they are incapable of doing anything perfectly. With spouses who are critical of each other, I require them to cease and desist with all criticisms and channel their hurt and anger toward their partner into a request for behavior change.

Trivializing your spouse's feelings, views, goals, hopes, wishes, and successes is also to be avoided at all costs. We married folks need to think twice before we say things like, "You shouldn't be sad about not getting that promotion," "Your view on that issue is shallow and uninformed," or "Don't think for one minute that you have what it takes to become a senior partner at work." When a spouse is willing to take the risk of sharing their feelings, thoughts, and aspirations with us, we need to accept them as they are and encourage them to keep opening up to us. If we are doing it right, our spouse will share their "inner world" with us so that we can get to know them better, and trivializing what they share is the surest way to get them to shut off the flow of inner-world material.

Rationalizing your bad behavior in a marriage is also the kiss of death to trust, safety, and intimacy. A quote I heard a long time ago that challenges me to this day is, "There's never a right reason for wrong behavior." When you mistreat your spouse, do not try to justify it. There is no justification for mistreating your spouse. Only the grossly immature among us say things like, "Well, they put me down, so it was okay for me to put them down." I tell my couples, "There are *reasons* you mistreat your spouse but never any excuses." When you mess up and wound your spouse, admit you did something wrong, do not make any excuses, do not justify it by pointing out how they hurt you, ask them to forgive you, and show them you are sorry by stopping the misbehavior.

Words are like punches, and some of us have become far too complacent about how many verbal punches we throw at our spouse. What you say and how you say it are huge deals in marriage, and all of us need to be more careful when it comes to the words we say, the tone we express them with, and how they affect our spouse.

Some Final Thoughts

Trash talking seems to be the norm these days. You see it across all aspects of life—politics, religion, and sports, just to name a few. Some people pride themselves on who can be the most creative, artistic, and deadliest trash-talker of all. What the best trash-talkers do not really understand is that they are demeaning another human being in the process, contributing to that person finding it harder to get through life in a psychologically healthy manner, and triggering feelings of shame and worthlessness.

As spouses, we need to speak wholesome words to each other, words that build up and don't tear down. We need to say words that reflect we are giving them our undivided attention, appreciate the positive things they do, affirm their positive character qualities, comfort them when they are sad, encourage them when they are discouraged, respect them as the image-bearer of God, and understand their deepest thoughts and feelings.

The way spouses sometimes talk to each other in this day and age bothers me. It is, far too often, the opposite of the words a spouse needs to hear. There are times I wish we could all go back to the time of Jane Austen and talk to each other in the mannered and civil way they did back then. I know that is not going to happen and that our level of discourse is probably going to get even worse over time, but it would be nice if we could return to a more civilized way of speaking.

Every so often, I will watch *Sense and Sensibility* or *Pride and Prejudice* just to listen to the dialogue. (I keep the remote in my hand in case Holly comes into the room and I need to quickly switch to a football game.) Man, oh man, is the level of conversation inspiring. I could listen to that kind of talk all day. I know, people back then were not perfect by any stretch of the imagination, but they sure seemed to keep their standards high when it came to how they talked to each other.

Do everything you can to talk to your spouse in a respectful, civil, and decent manner. Set the bar high when it comes to the words you say to each other and the tone with which you say them. When your words or tone are abusive, own it, apologize, ask for forgiveness, and keep working to comply with the command, "Do not let any unwholesome talk come out of your mouths, but only what is helpful for building others up according to their needs, that it may benefit those who listen" (Eph. 4:29). You will not regret it.

Here's a loving reminder to keep doing the workbook, especially with regard to this chapter.

CHAPTER EIGHT

Shoot Straight for Their Good

We are all travelers in the wilderness of this world, and the best we can find in our travels is an honest friend.

—Robert Louis Stevenson

Instead, speaking the truth in love, we will grow to become in every respect the mature body of him who is the head, that is, Christ.

—Ephesians 4:15

In a national television commercial, the spokesperson for an insurance company, after asking whether their company can save you money, posed the question, "Was Abe Lincoln honest?" The commercial goes on to show a supposed interaction "Honest Abe" had with his wife, Mary, where she asks him, "Does this dress make my backside look big?"

Lincoln anxiously fumbles around for a few seconds before saying, "Perhaps a . . ." as he makes the hand gesture indicating "just a little," his thumb and index finger held a tiny bit apart. Mary thanks him for his honesty by storming out of the room, leaving her husband flustered and anxious about what just occurred in their marriage.

The principle we focused on in the last chapter had to do with how not to talk to your spouse. We went into my counseling office and looked at a couple that frequently talked trash to each other, much to the detriment of their marriage. We then went into fourteen different ways we fall into being verbally abusive to our spouse, many of which this couple was actively practicing. In this chapter, we are going to talk about how important it is to comply with the principle "speaking the truth in love" (Eph. 4:15) for a marriage to flourish.

Before we do that, let's go back into my office and look at a couple who was doing the opposite—speaking falsehoods out of bitterness and resentment toward each other. Sadly, it is not uncommon for couples to distort the reality of who their spouse is and then throw that distorted picture in their face in an effort to punish and hurt. Good couples counseling is marked by many things, but it is certainly marked by helping a couple turn from speaking mistruths in anger to speaking the truth in love.

"That's Not True!"

Randy and Denise met in a singles class at church when they were in their mid-twenties. Both came from families that were hypercritical and shaming. They left those families wondering if there was anything good about themselves, anything that went in the "plus" column when it came to having positive traits or qualities.

During the time they dated, Randy and Denise were careful not to add further fuel to the fire and avoided making critical remarks about each other. Neither wanted to do anything that would blow the relationship up and keep them from walking down the aisle. After they got married, it was a much different story.

By the time they came to see me, the marriage had turned into a critical and shaming nightmare, and neither Randy nor Denise felt they could trust the feedback the other was giving. They saw their spouse as constantly distorting the reality of who they really were, and they ultimately shut their ears to hearing each other's feedback.

"We never agree with what the other says. I don't trust Randy's view of me at all, and I think he's constantly putting his negative qualities off on me. I simply don't listen to anything he has to say anymore," Denise says, starting off our first session.

"I don't think you hear anything I say because you don't want to face the things about you that are bad," Randy responds.

"I'm happy to hear feedback but not when you seem so determined to put me down in the process. I don't feel like your motives for bringing things to my attention are healthy . . . I think you just want to put me down and make me feel small," Denise replies.

"I could say the same thing about you. The way you talk about me leaves me wondering if you know me at all; it's always so negative. And I sure don't feel you give me feedback because you care about me . . . I think you give me feedback because you're angry and want to belittle me," Randy shoots back.

"I don't think either of us sees the other accurately, and I sure don't feel that our intentions are good when we give each other input," Denise answers.

"I agree," Randy replies.

"Could each of you give me an example of what you're talking about?" I ask.

"Sure. Just the other day, Randy came to me and said I never follow through on anything just because I didn't follow through on going grocery shopping for us that night. For him to use the word 'never' when talking about me triggered not feeling safe with him, given that I knew it wasn't true. And saying it that way, I knew he wasn't being loving in why he said it," Denise answers.

"Randy, what comes to mind for you?" I ask.

"A few weeks back, I went out with some of my buddies to see a movie. You would have thought I shot the Pope! Denise told me that all I ever think about is myself. That's simply not true, and I sure didn't appreciate her describing me that way. It felt like she was purposely being negative about me because she feels hurt that I don't spend every waking moment with her. Why would I want to spend time with her if that's how negative of a view she has of me?" Randy says.

"Let me ask you both something. Are you hearing the two things in your interactions with each other that are hurtful to you?"

"Well, I'm hearing one thing for sure . . . that neither of us feels the other sees us for who we really are . . . that when we say something, it's a distorted view of each other," Denise replies.

"Yeah, I'm hearing that, too" I answer.

"The thing I'm hearing is that both of us feel the other says what they do to be hurtful, to wound each other," Randy adds.

"Yeah, I'm hearing that as well," I reply.

"Not a very pretty picture, is it?" Denise says.

"No, not a very pretty picture. But I think we can work on those two things . . . being more accurate in what you say to each other and doing it out of a motive to love each other . . . and turn your marriage around. Are you game?" I ask.

"Yes."

"Yes."

The three of us worked diligently on improving those two things in their marriage—being more accurate in their feedback and giving feedback out of a desire to help each other grow into better people. There were a lot of stops and starts, given how deeply entrenched they were in giving inaccurate feedback out of desire to wound each other, but Randy and Denise did not flinch in their dedication to improve in this area of their marriage.

Am I speaking falsehoods out of meanness or speaking the truth out of love? Every one of us, me included, needs to ask that question of ourselves each and every day if we are going to become the kind of spouse God wants us to be. If we truly want our spouse to hear us, we have to meet these two criteria in what we say and why we say it. Even then, given how fallen we are, it will be hard to hear feedback from each other, but we are at least making it more likely that healthy communication will occur.

Four Ways to Speak to Your Spouse, Only One of Which Is Healthy

I want to walk you through four options we have for how to speak to our spouse, only one of which is the loving way to do it. The first three are how *not* to do it when you are the one giving feedback to your spouse. The fourth one is the path to marital harmony and closeness.

Speak a Lie in Love

Here you are not being accurate in what you are saying to your spouse but talking to them out of a genuine desire to love them. An example would be saying something like, "You *never* let me finish a sentence. I'm telling you this because I care about you and want us to become better communicators." The first sentence is a lie; the second sentence shows a desire for connection.

Speak the Truth in Hate

Here you are being accurate in how you describe your spouse but doing it out of a desire to condemn, demean, and denigrate. An example would be saying something like, "You *sometimes* interrupt me before I'm done talking, and frankly I'm sick and tired of you being such a jerk!" The first part of the sentence is true, and the second part just drives home the desire to hurt.

Speak a Lie in Hate

This is the worst combination of all. Here you are not only being inaccurate in how you describe your spouse, but you are doing it out of a desire to be mean and hurtful. An example would be saying something like, "You never let me finish a sentence, and frankly I'm getting sick and tired of you being such a jerk!" This statement begins with a lie and ends with lashing out.

Speak the Truth in Love

This is the best combination of all because it is checking off both biblical boxes—you are being accurate in what you say (truthful) and doing it out of a desire to foster your spouse's growth as a human being (loving). An example would be saying something like, "You sometimes interrupt me before I'm done talking, and I'm bringing this to your attention because I want both of us to be better communicators in our marriage." This way you make a true statement and also suggest change in a loving way.

Far too many couples bounce around like a pinball between the first three options. What is rare is for a couple to get into a regular habit of speaking the truth in love. The reason this is rare is because we humans have a fallen tendency to mentally distort the reality of who our spouse is and react to them out of self-righteous punitiveness when they do not act the way we want them to.

This is why I want you to turn to God for help to become a "speak the truth in love" kind of spouse. Your human effort to become this kind of spouse is simply not going to be enough. Do not forget: "God is working in you, giving you the desire and the power to do what pleases him" (Phil. 2:13 NLT). It is God who gives you the desire and the power to become a more loving spouse—do not try to give that to yourself.

The "Shoot Straight for Their Good" Marriage

Bringing a spouse's flaws to their attention is risky business, especially if you do not start with an honest examination of your own shortcomings in the marriage. Nevertheless, marriage is supposed to be a relationship in which "as iron sharpens iron, so one person sharpens another" (Prov. 27:17), and it requires we take that risk.

While there are certainly exceptions to the rule, your spouse is the one person on the planet who knows you better than most. Your spouse is the one person who has been around you 24/7 over the years. It is not uncommon in marriage for your spouse to have a more accurate view of you than you do of yourself. Consequently, your spouse is often in the best position to hold up a mirror showing the things you need to change.

Trying to hold up this mirror comes with great risk because all spouses have a somewhat distorted view of each other. No spouse sees their partner for who they truly are. Every spouse misperceives the reality of their partner's good, bad, and ugly qualities. So why should we allow a spouse to weigh in on who we are and give us corrective feedback? All I can tell you is that if you do not open up to your spouse being honest with you about your flaws and defects, you are shutting off a rich source of input that could be helpful in your efforts to get your act together and become a mature adult.

Along these lines, I would encourage you to do something counterintuitive in marriage. Instead of being the kind of spouse who does not want their partner's input or who gets defensive when it is offered, *seek it*. Go to your spouse two or three times a week and ask them the following question: "How can I become a better person and treat you in a more loving way?" First, you will have to pick them up off the floor because they certainly will not have seen that coming. Second, you will be showing them that being married to you is going to be an iron-sharpening-iron experience where feedback is sought rather than resisted and appreciated rather than resented. Finally, it might inspire your spouse to lower their defensive shields when it comes to receiving input from you, and they might choose to let the marriage help them grow into a more loving and mature person as well.

All this might sound good in theory, but I can assure you it is great if you will practice it. I have seen numerous marriages turn completely around because a couple committed to *seeking* each other's input on how to improve their relationship rather than *running* from it. It may not seem like it is worth the risk, but it is. You may not trust that your partner will give you feedback that is accurate and loving, but I want you to give it a try and see whether the results turn out better than you thought possible.

When you seek your spouse's input, resolve in your mind and heart that you are going to take everything they say *seriously,* but only take to heart the part that is true. Also, hear what they have to say even if it might be coming from a bitter or resentful place in their heart. Even the most inaccurate and mean-spirited feedback from a spouse has some truth to it that is worth considering.

Take the risk. Seek your spouse's feedback on a regular basis, take to heart the parts that are true, and keep working on becoming a more loving partner "as long as you both shall live."

Some Final Thoughts

In a healthy marriage, we need to shoot straight for our spouse's good by providing them with accurate feedback aimed at fostering their growth. This is a hard thing to risk, given that none of us is perfect, and we frequently need to get that kind of feedback ourselves.

Related to this, I am reminded of Proverbs 27:5–6: "Better is open rebuke than hidden love. Wounds from a friend can be trusted, but an enemy multiplies kisses." I could be misinterpreting these verses, but I think they are saying that if someone is a *true friend* they will openly speak the truth to you even though you may find it hurtful. Conversely, a person is not being a true friend if they "multiply kisses" and only tell you the things you want to hear.

Let's steward our marriages by being willing to speak the truth in love to our spouse when prompted by God to do so. Notice I said "when prompted by God." You do not want to prompt yourself to speak to your spouse. If you do that, you are more likely to make a real mess of the interaction. Let God be the one to prompt you to say something, help you be accurate in what you say, and help you bring concerns to their attention out of a loving desire to help them grow into the person God wants them to be.

CHAPTER NINE

Wipe the Slate Clean

When we forgive, we set a prisoner free and discover that the prisoner we set free is us.

—Lewis B. Smedes

Bear with each other and forgive one another if any of you has a grievance against someone.

—Colossians 3:13

A Minneapolis couple decided to go to Florida to thaw out during a particularly cold winter. They planned to stay at the same hotel where they spent their honeymoon thirty years earlier. Because of their hectic schedules, it was difficult for the couple to coordinate their travel plans. So the husband left Minnesota and flew to Florida on Thursday, while his wife planned to fly down the next day.

The husband checked into the hotel. There was a computer in his room, so he decided to send an email to his wife. However, he accidentally left out one letter of her email address and sent the email without realizing his error.

Meanwhile, somewhere in Houston, a widow had just returned home from her husband's funeral. He was a minister who was called home to glory following a heart attack. The widow decided to check her email, expecting condolences from family and friends. But after reading her very first email, she screamed and fainted. The widow's son rushed into the room, found his mother on the floor, and saw the computer screen which read:

> *To: My Loving Wife*
> *Subject: I've Just Arrived Today*
>
> *I know you're surprised to hear from me. They have computers here now and you are allowed to send emails to your loved ones. Since I've just arrived, I thought I would send you an email. Everything has been prepared for your arrival tomorrow. Looking forward to seeing you then! Hope your journey is as uneventful as mine was.*
>
> *P.S. Sure is hot down here!!!*

The husband in this story was trying to be loving toward his wife, but because he left out one letter of her email address, he almost sent a grieving widow to an early grave. After the widow was revived, she probably needed to "speak the truth in love" to the erring husband to help him see what he had done. If the erring husband was humble, he would have profusely apologized for his mistake, asked for her forgiveness, and sent the email to his wife to let her know what had happened. If everyone was in their right mind, they all could have enjoyed a good belly laugh and moved on.

In marriage, we sometimes get wounded by our spouse in rather egregious ways (the big four in Scripture are adultery, abandonment, neglect, and abuse). But most of the time, we are wounded by our spouse in smaller ways, like them forgetting to do something they said they would do, not pursuing quality time with us, and not properly sharing the workload around the house or with the kids. Whatever the size of the wound, all of us are going to feel hurt by our spouse along the way, and consequently we all need to forgive in order for a marriage to heal.

The origins of this quote are not known for sure, but one astute observer of humankind noted, "Unforgiveness is like drinking poison and hoping the other person dies." Hard to argue with that, isn't it? There is something inside of every human being that struggles to forgive others when they wound us. We actually think we are getting the other person back if we withhold forgiveness, only to realize that unforgiveness is a poison killing us from within.

In this chapter, I will focus on the struggle many of us have to forgive, to wipe the slate clean when our spouse mistreats us. I have seen marriages go down the tubes for various reasons, but I would put the unwillingness to forgive in the top three for why marriages end in divorce. To get along well with our spouse, we absolutely, nonnegotiably must forgive our spouse when they hurt us. No marriage can afford an unforgiving heart. If we bitterly hold a grudge against our spouse and resent them for the ways they mistreat us, the marriage is toast. No two people can get along if either of them chooses to drink the poison of unforgiveness.

The Wife Who Refused to Forgive

Marianne had looked forward her whole life to finding and marrying the man of her dreams. She kissed a lot of frogs along the way, but none of them turned into a prince until she met Allen. Allen was everything she ever wanted in a man. Though certainly not perfect, Allen was a cut above the rest when it came to the kind of men Marianne dated in high school and college. He was hardworking, responsible, understanding, kind, funny, ambitious, and passionate about his faith. Marianne knew from the minute she met Allen that he was the man for her, something that was only further confirmed during the year and a half they dated.

Marianne and Allen did it right. They took their time getting to know each other and worked on having a strong friendship at the heart of their relationship. They asked each other a lot of tough questions, were courageous enough to give each other honest answers, and got to know each other's heart at a deep and transparent level.

One day, about three or four years into their marriage, Marianne noticed Allen had left his laptop open on the kitchen table. Out of curiosity, she looked through his search history and found a lengthy list of porn sites he had visited. Marianne was devastated. Rather than keep it "in house" at first by going to Allen directly, she told her mother and sister what had happened and got their input on what she should do about it. Her mother and sister, furious with Allen for what he had done, told Marianne she needed to confront him, kick him out of the house, and demand he go see someone for help. That is exactly what she did. Allen owned up to what he did and was honest about having had a struggle with pornography since high school. Marianne was enraged he had kept this from her, especially since she had asked him about it when they dated.

Allen was unwilling to leave their home even though Marianne demanded he do so. He felt Marianne was weaponizing her hurt and anger as a battering ram against him and being shaming and punitive in how she was treating him. He started sleeping in a spare bedroom, but the two of them rarely spoke and decided to reach out for some help.

"Dr. Thurman, I'm devastated by what Allen has done. He lied to me when we were dating about whether or not he looked at porn, and he's been lying to me about it the whole time we've been married. I would have never married him if I had known he was addicted to porn. I feel sick to my stomach every time I look at him, and I don't know what to do," Marianne starts off the session, tears streaming down her face.

"Can you tell me more about how you feel about it?" I ask.

"The only word I can think of is *devastated*—I'm devastated he would do such a dark, evil thing and cover it up the whole time we've been together. My stomach is in a knot all the time, I can't concentrate at work, I dread coming home, and he won't leave the house to give me some space," she offers.

"Dr. Thurman, I've owned up to what I did, and I've asked Marianne to forgive me. I understand why she is hurt and angry about this, and rightly so. I have been lying to her about looking at porn the whole time we've been together. This area of my life is something I feel so ashamed about that I haven't been willing to tell anyone. It was wrong of me to hide this from her. Not telling Marianne about it kept her from knowing something about me that might have led to her moving on from our relationship. Selfishly, I wasn't willing to risk that," Allen admits.

"No, you weren't willing to risk losing me, and you did keep me from knowing some things about you that would have kept me from marrying you. You deceived me, and I feel I've made a commitment to a man that

I no longer respect or want to be around. You say you're a Christian, but you sure don't look like one to me!" Marianne adds, further shaming Allen for his struggle.

"I wish I could undo the past, Dr. Thurman. I really do. It wasn't right for me to keep this from her. She needed to know this about me so she could make a choice that was best for her in terms of moving on from me or not. It's no wonder she doesn't have any respect for me. I get that," Allen says.

"I would hope you do! Now I'm stuck with someone I can't stand, and each day feels like I'm being tortured being around you. I would never have done this to you . . . never!" she adds.

"Marianne, it's certainly understandable you feel deeply hurt and angry about Allen's struggle with pornography. I would be concerned about you if you weren't. In here, I'm going to give you all the room you need to express what you're feeling so you can decide what you want to do about it," I offer.

"Thank you, Dr. Thurman. I appreciate that," she responds.

"I want you to try to hear this next thing as best you can. Whether you decide to stay with Allen or not, I strongly encourage you to forgive him. The last thing you want to do the rest of your life is carry around unforgiveness and bitterness toward Allen, something that would only poison your own soul and make it hard for you to truly move on, with him or without him," I respond.

"You're not telling me I need to forgive him right now, are you? There's no way that's going to happen," she responds.

"No, not at all. For forgiveness to be genuine, it has to be something we work on over time. So, no, I'm not telling you to forgive him today, but I'm cautioning you that if you're not careful, you won't ever forgive him. That would only make your life miserable, keep you from growing into a more mature and loving person, and get in the way of future relationships being healthy and good," I counter.

"Well, I'm certainly not ready to forgive him yet. I don't know if I will ever be," she admits.

"Dr. Thurman, I get it that it is hard for Marianne to forgive me for what I did. But I've got to be honest, I'm not going to stay married to someone who won't forgive me, especially given that I've admitted what I've done is wrong and am getting some help," Allen adds.

"Is that a threat?" Marianne fires back.

"No, it's not a threat. I'm just saying it's understandable you're deeply hurt and having a hard time forgiving me, but I'm not going to let you spend the rest of our marriage punishing me for it," Allen responds, putting his own boundaries in place with Marianne for the kind of marriage he is willing to accept.

"Then leave! Move out and never come back! I'll be a lot happier without you!" Marianne responds, bitterness dripping from every word.

"Let me jump in here. I know this is hard to hear right now, but every marriage goes through times of deep wounding. To heal from those wounds, two things have to occur. First, the person who did the offense has to be genuinely sorry they did it and stop doing it. Second, the offended person has to forgive. If either person refuses to do their part, the marriage can't heal and healthily move on," I offer.

"Well, I'm doing my part . . . I've taken responsibility for lying to Marianne, I'm genuinely sorry for hurting her, and I'm getting some help. I know she isn't there yet, but I'm worried she won't ever forgive me," Allen says with fear in his voice.

"I might not. Some things are unforgivable," she replies.

Marianne and Allen were in a bad place. Marianne was deeply wounded by what Allen had done and was having a hard time deciding whether she would ever forgive him and let him back in her heart. Allen understood how deeply he had hurt Marianne, and it seemed to me he was genuinely sorry for what he had done. He was working hard in counseling to deal with his addiction to pornography so he could be a healthier person and a safer, more loving partner to his wife.

Sadly, no matter how hard Allen worked on his own issues, Marianne continued to let bitterness and resentment fill her soul. She continued to see Allen's struggle with pornography as the only issue in the marriage and the thing that irreparably damaged it. Marianne decided to file for divorce to force Allen to move out. They stopped coming to see me and divorced six months later. This is always heartbreaking given that both people can, if they are willing, do their part to repair even the deepest ruptures in marriage and make it even stronger than before.

I do not want you to read this as me putting the demise of the marriage all on Marianne. What I hope you are hearing is that, in this case, it was Marianne's unwillingness to forgive Allen that made the marriage impossible to repair. In spite of my best efforts to encourage her to forgive, she refused. Allen, though heartbroken, knew the marriage was not tenable if she was going to continue to act out her hurt and anger by being rejecting and punitive toward him about what he had done.

From a spiritual warfare perspective, the enemy won this one. The enemy was able to take someone's understandable hurt and anger and turn it into bitterness, resentment, and contempt toward their spouse. The enemy was able to take someone's bitterness and blind them to their own fallenness as a human being before a holy God. This breaks my heart because so many good and wonderful things were waiting on Marianne and Allen if both had done their part to heal and restore the marriage.

The Unbiblical Reasons We Don't Forgive in Marriage

Let's talk for a minute about the reasons we choose not to forgive our spouse when they wound us. Given that being unforgiving is like drinking poison, it is always a self-injurious act when we do not forgive and reflective of a faulty view of what forgiveness is all about. Here are the primary *unbiblical* reasons we choose to withhold forgiveness from our spouse when they wound us.

They Have to Earn My Forgiveness

Forgiveness is not something a spouse should have to earn. Forgiveness is a matter of grace, wiping the slate clean and not requiring them to do anything to earn it. God did not ask us to earn his forgiveness. His forgiveness of us was offered as a free gift that we did nothing to merit. That is how we are supposed to think about forgiving our spouse when they hurt us.

They Are Not Sorry

There are times we withhold forgiveness because our spouse is not sorry for what they did. We are commanded to forgive others whether they are sorry for what they did or not. And in some cases, we will wait the rest of our lives for our spouse to be genuinely sorry about how they hurt us. Forgiveness is an unmerited act of the will and does not depend on a spouse being sorry for hurting us.

They Are Going to Hurt Me Again

We sometimes withhold forgiveness because a spouse might hurt us again. The truth of the matter is that our spouse will hurt us again in the future—plan on it. But it is never a reason to withhold forgiveness. Marriage is a contact sport, and you can be sure your spouse will wound you at times, sometimes in the same way. We are to forgive "seventy-seven times" (Matt. 18:22), which means an unlimited number of times, whether they hurt us that way again or not. We will talk about this later, but if our spouse continues to sin so that grace may abound, we need to implement firm boundaries to protect ourselves. But we are never to withhold forgiveness.

I Have to Let Them Back into My Life

Forgiveness does not automatically mean you reconcile with your spouse. If your spouse wounds you and is not sorry, you have every reason to assertively keep them at arm's length until they change their ways. You are supposed to forgive a spouse no matter what they do, but reconciliation depends on them doing their part by turning from their hurtful actions.

It Means I'm Saying That What They Did Was No Big Deal

Small wounds spouses inflict on each other *are* no big deal and do not warrant forgiveness. For example, let's say your spouse, on occasion, interrupts you before you finish a sentence. Something like that is minor and does not require forgiveness. When you forgive, it means that your spouse did something that was a *big deal.* For example, let's say your spouse opens up a private charge card account and gets the two of you in $25,000 of charge card debt. That is a big enough deal to require forgiveness. We do not forgive a spouse for the tiny nicks and bruises they inflict on us. We forgive them for the deeper cuts and bruises they inflict. When you forgive someone, you are saying that what they did was a *big deal.*

It Means I Am Letting Them Get Away with What They Did

A spouse never "gets away" with mistreating you. If they have a conscience, they pay for what they did by feeling guilty and miserable in their soul. If they do not have a conscience (a sociopath), they pay for what they did on the day they stand before God and have to give an account for their actions. No spouse ultimately gets away with wrongdoing. One way or another, we all pay for wounding our spouse, either on this side of heaven or the other. It is not our job to be our spouse's judge, jury, and executioner and make them pay for wounding us. We leave our spouse's gross misdeeds up to God because he will handle them in a much healthier and appropriate manner than we would. But do not forget: Have firm boundaries with your spouse to healthily protect yourself from their wrongdoing.

You Do Not Realize How Much You Have Been Forgiven

When we withhold forgiveness, we are in denial about how much God has forgiven us, given all the sinful things we have done. Being unwilling to forgive means we are taking on an air of moral superiority and self-righteousness toward our spouse, as if they are so much worse than we are. We all fall short of the moral perfection and holiness of God, way far short, and we do not want to stomp around our marriage acting as if we are better than our spouse. We are not. People in glass houses should never throw stones, and we all live in glass houses. Try not to forget how much God has forgiven you. It will make it a lot easier to forgive your spouse.

There are no *legitimate* reasons to withhold forgiveness in marriage, only illegitimate ones. We forgive our spouse because we have been forgiven by God. We do not make them earn it, nor do we require that they are sorry for what they did. We do not withhold forgiveness because our spouse might hurt us again, nor do we immediately reconcile with our spouse just because we have forgiven them. We do not buy into the lie that forgiving a spouse means we are saying what they did was no big deal, and we leave our spouse's actions up to a holy God for his discipline. We humbly stay close to the fact that "all have sinned and fall short of the glory of God" (Rom. 3:23) and that we ourselves stand in need of forgiveness.

The "Wipe the Slate Clean" Marriage

Every day of marriage seems to bring another wound or hurt along with it. We need to be discerning about which hurts are serious enough to warrant forgiveness and which hurts need to be water off a duck's back. When the wound is a serious one, it is a lot easier to think about forgiving our spouse than to actually do it. Nevertheless, throughout the course of our marriages, we are going to be given numerous opportunities to become more forgiving people.

A few of words of clarification about forgiveness in marriage.

First, do not tell your spouse you have forgiven them. Forgiving your spouse for hurting you is an internal accomplishment and needs to be kept to yourself unless your spouse asks. If your spouse asks if you have forgiven them for something they did, be honest about it. If you have not forgiven them, be honest enough to say, "I haven't gotten there yet, but I'm working on it." If you have, tell them, "Yes, with God's help, I have forgiven you for what you did, have wiped the slate clean, and have put that in the past." Wherever you are on the matter, let your spouse know you are trying to allow God to help you become a genuinely forgiving spouse who does not allow bitterness and resentment to run the show.

Second, do not justify withholding forgiveness from your spouse. As I have already discussed, there are no legitimate reasons for being unforgiving, and you are only poisoning yourself when you choose not to forgive your spouse. As I said earlier, "There's never a right reason for wrong behavior," and being unforgiving is wrong behavior. If you are unwilling to forgive your spouse, own up to that being a character defect in you, not a statement about how much they hurt you.

Finally, do not ever forget you stand in need of forgiveness in your marriage as well. Sometimes, we focus so much on how our spouse hurts us that we do not see how often we hurt them. We are just as fallen as the person we are married to, and we need to eat our daily helping of humble pie about that being true. Poet George Herbert put it beautifully when he said, "He that cannot forgive others breaks the bridge over which he himself must pass if he would ever reach heaven; for everyone has need to be forgiven."

Each day of marriage presents another opportunity to wipe the slate clean and forgive our spouse for the hurtful things they do. Consequently, each day of marriage presents another opportunity to mature into a whole and loving person. Forgiving your spouse is as much for your growth, development, and well-being as anything else. Forgive your spouse when they wound you because, as Lewis Smedes noted at the top of this chapter, you are setting a prisoner free that happens to be you.

Some Final Thoughts

I have had people in my office who were healthy and humble enough to forgive their spouse for some grievous things. And I have had people in my office who were pathological and prideful enough to be unwilling to forgive their spouse for the pettiest of things. We all stand in need of forgiveness, and we all need to forgive our spouse when they hurt us. As with everything else in this book, all this is easier said than done, but if we want to get along well with our spouse, we need to do it.

The quote by Lewis Smedes that opened this chapter cuts in two directions. When you will not forgive your spouse for how they hurt you, you make yourself a prisoner and cannot experience true freedom in your marriage. When you do not seek their forgiveness for how you hurt them, you also make yourself a prisoner and cannot experience true freedom in your marriage. I would take the liberty of modifying his quote by saying, "When we forgive our spouse and ask them to forgive us, we set a prisoner free and discover that the prisoner we set free was us."

Refusing to forgive in marriage is a choice we make, and it dooms us to a life of bitterness, resentment, and victimhood. Not for one single second do I believe people when they say they *can't* forgive their spouse for hurting them. I empathize with how hard it can be to forgive, especially the darkest wrongs done to us, but we need to drop the word "can't" out of our vocabulary and replace it with "won't." We are willfully breaking the bridge over which we must cross when we refuse to forgive our spouse.

Do you want to be set free in your relationship with your spouse? If you do, you need to forgive them when they hurt you, and you need to ask them to forgive you when you mess up. Choose to forgive and seek to be forgiven. There is no other way to experience the true freedom you were meant to have in marriage.

CHAPTER TEN

Tell on Yourself

In the confession of concrete sins the old man dies a painful, shameful death before the eyes of a brother. Because this humiliation is so hard, we continually scheme to avoid it. Yet in the deep mental and physical pain of humiliation before a brother we experience our rescue and salvation.

—Dietrich Bonhoeffer

Therefore confess your sins to each other and pray for each other so that you may be healed.

—James 5:16

Ed and Carolyn met while on a singles cruise, and Ed fell head over heels for her. When they discovered they lived in the same city only a few miles apart, Ed was ecstatic. He immediately started asking her out when they got home. Within a couple of weeks, Ed had taken Carolyn to dance clubs, restaurants, concerts, movies, and museums. Ed became convinced that Carolyn was indeed his soulmate and true love. Every date seemed better than the last.

On the one-month anniversary of their first dinner on the cruise ship, Ed took Carolyn to a fine restaurant. While having cocktails and waiting for their salad, Ed said, "I guess you can tell I'm very much in love with you.

I'd like to have a serious talk before our relationship continues to the next stage. So, before I get a box out of my jacket and ask you a life-changing question, it's only fair to warn you, I'm a total golf nut. I play golf; I read about golf; I watch golf on TV. In short, I eat, sleep, and breathe golf. If that's going to be a problem for us, you'd better say so now!"

Carolyn took a deep breath and responded, "Ed, that certainly won't be a problem. I love you as you are and I love golf, too. But, since we're being totally honest with each other, you need to know that for the last five years I've . . . I've been a hooker."

"That's alright," Ed said. "I bet it's because you're not keeping your wrists straight when you hit the ball."

We have a lot of expressions in counseling. One of the most important is, "You're only as sick as your secrets." For us to experience true closeness with our spouse, we must take the mask off we use to cover up the things we feel ashamed of and find the courage to get real. We have to tell on ourselves.

Unfortunately, few of us seem willing to take that risk. Given the negative reactions we sometimes get when we open up about our most painful struggles, I do not really blame us. Stop for a minute and think about whether there is anyone in your life you feel safe enough to tell *everything* about the struggles you have, someone to whom you could expose the darkest parts of who you are and not worry they would react in a denigrating or condemning manner. Not many of us have that kind of person in our lives. Even when we do, some of us still hesitate to come out from behind our "I'm doing just fine" mask and let them help us break free from the struggles we have as we go through life.

Theoretically, our spouse is supposed to be the one we can take our mask off with and reveal our deepest, darkest stuff to. I have not witnessed very many marriages inside or outside my office where this is the case. Far too many marriages are not safe places for "keeping it real," and so a lot of us hide in our marriages and act like the difficult struggles we are dealing with are relatively minor and nothing to worry about.

I am not suggesting you tell absolutely everything to your spouse. I think we have to be wise and discerning when it comes to what we tell our spouse. In the grand scheme of things, if we feel it wise to withhold certain things from our spouse, we need to make sure we are telling someone—a counselor, trusted friend, seasoned pastor, and the like.

I have witnessed more than a few marriages where spouses kept things from each other that needed to be confessed. As a result, everyone was walking around carrying secrets that made the marriage "sick" in the sense of not being a place of honesty, transparency, and humility. Let me take you into my counseling office to give you an example.

The Millionaire Who Was Not Worth a Penny

Ted was a senior partner at a prestigious law firm where he had been very successful financially, or so everyone thought. The surface reason he gave for coming to see me was that he wanted to talk about how his wife, Cindy, constantly questioned him about whether or not he was being honest about their financial situation.

Ted and Cindy had a lavish lifestyle, spent money in ways that most of us could only dream of, and seemed to be sailing through life without a worry in the world. Nevertheless, Cindy's "spider sense" led her to believe that Ted was not being honest with her about how things were going financially, and she was suspicious they were not doing as well as he suggested.

Right from the start in my work with Ted, my curiosity was piqued about how he was really doing financially, given that he became defensive when I questioned him about it. His overly strong reaction to being asked about his finances made me wonder if he was hiding something. Nevertheless, you start every client off with a clean slate, go where they want to take you, and hope and pray they are telling you the truth.

"It bugs the heck out of me that Cindy questions me about our finances and doesn't trust what I say."

"You have any guesses as to why?"

"Not really. She just doesn't trust me when I tell her we're doing great."

"Could she be picking up on something about your finances that makes her wonder if you are being honest?"

"What do you mean?"

"Well, my experience with a lot of couples over the years is that spouses often have a spider-sense when something is going on with their partner . . . that they pick up on things happening behind the scenes that their spouse is afraid to tell them about. So, let me ask you directly, how are you guys doing financially?"

"Great! We've never been better!"

"So, things are going really well?"

"Absolutely. I just wish Cindy would trust me about it and stop pressuring me to prove we're doing fine."

"Has she done that?"

"Done what?"

"Asked you to show her your finances, bank accounts, savings, and retirement to prove you guys are doing well?"

"Yes."

"Do you?"

"No . . . it's too complicated to explain to her and would be a complete waste of time."

"When you won't show her how you are doing financially, how does she react?"

"She gets more anxious about it, questions me even more, and makes it clear she doesn't trust a word I'm saying."

"Where do things go from there?"

"I usually storm out of the room."

"So, this issue never gets resolved. She doesn't trust that you're telling her the truth, and you get angry when she doesn't believe you."

"Exactly. If she would just get off my back about it, we would get along a whole lot better."

"But she isn't going to get off your back because she thinks you're not shooting straight with her. And if she thinks you guys are struggling financially, she probably isn't going to be able to calm down about it, right?"

"Right."

"So, why don't you prove to her that things are going well financially? In the end, wouldn't it save the two of you a lot of wasted time and energy?"

"Look, it wouldn't do any good. If I took her into every detail of our financial situation, she would still think I'm hiding things from her. There is nothing I can say or do that is going to calm her down . . . nothing! The pressure I'm under at work is intense, and I don't have the energy to get her to believe me. She should just take what I say at face value!"

"So, it sounds like the two of you are in a standoff and that this issue in your marriage is never going to go away."

"Yeah, I guess you're right. Isn't there anything I can do?" Ted asks.

"Well, it seems to me you have three options. First, you can continue to be defensive about it and storm out of the room when she presses you about your finances. That option doesn't work, but you're free to keep doing it. Second, you can take a lie detector test where she gets to come up with the questions you are asked. Third, you can give her complete, unfettered access to your financial situation, with a forensic accountant alongside that both of you trust, and you can let the cards fall where they may."

"Well, I'm not willing to do the second and third options, so I guess I'm stuck with option number one—a wife who is always on my back about finances, who doesn't trust anything I say about them, and who is going to drive me crazy the rest of my life when she ought to be thankful for the incredible lifestyle I've provided for her and the kids."

"Ted, I mean this with all due respect, but if you're not willing to do the second or third options, I can't help you."

"What do you mean? Can't I just come in here to talk about it?" he replies with a tone of desperation in his voice.

"Sure, I'm just saying I won't be able to help because you're unwilling to do what it takes to calm Cindy's concerns down. As long as that's your stance, counseling is not going to do you much good."

"Okay, I'll think about it."

Ted would come back in to see me every so often to talk about how frustrated he was that Cindy did not trust him, never talking about himself or anything that was going on with him that needed to change. He never took the extra step of proving to Cindy they were doing well financially, and Cindy never quit worrying they were living in a financial house of cards that might come tumbling down some day.

That day came. It turned out that Ted had been "robbing Peter to pay Paul" for years in dealings with financial investors and sunk his family into millions of dollars of debt. Ted had spent years enabling his family to have an extravagant lifestyle while privately getting deeper in debt and hiding it from everyone. His investors sued, he was found guilty in federal court of being engaged in a Ponzi scheme where he had defrauded investors of millions of dollars, and he was sent to prison for over ten years. He and his family had to sell off all their possessions and holdings to pay investors back, and they never returned to the lavish lifestyle they once led.

It breaks my heart when I think about Ted. He was a good-hearted man who loved his family and wanted everyone to enjoy life and live it fully. Sadly, he allowed the pressure he was under financially to lead him to cut corners in his financial dealings with others and fell deeper and deeper into a financial hole out of which he could never climb. The mistake Ted made along the way was to not tell anybody about it when things began to worsen, and the financial snowball that began to roll downhill finally crushed him as it got larger and gained speed.

Ted's shame, embarrassment, and ego led him to paint a rosy picture of great success to his wife, law partners, and friends while everything behind the scenes was anything but great. Ted experienced the reality of "you may be sure that your sin will find you out" (Num. 32:23), that you can run from problems but cannot ultimately hide, and it blew his world apart. When what he had been doing behind the scenes got exposed, it forced Ted to decide if he was going to keep covering things up and running from his problems or find the courage to tell the truth and face them. Ted decided to keep covering up and running, and, tragically, he did so all the way to prison.

When we keep our most grievous misdeeds and struggles hidden from others, we harm not only ourselves but those around us. If we want to get along better with others, especially our spouse, we need to come clean about the darkest wrongs we do and the deadliest character defects we have. We need to be transparent about the difficult things we battle in our day-to-day lives so that people can know us for who we really are and help us address the defective things inside of us rather than be destroyed by them. We need to make a choice to not allow shame and public embarrassment to cause us to hide our misdeeds from others, courageously pull the "I'm doing great" mask off, and ask for help.

The Five Kinds of "Tell on Yourself" Spouses

There are five basic styles of confessing your sins to your spouse. Four are unhealthy and damage your marriage, while one is healthy and can lead to a better, more meaningful level of closeness with your spouse. Think about which of these styles you might be bent toward and whether it has cost you a closer relationship with your spouse.

The "Nothing to Tell on Myself" Spouse

There are two versions of this kind of spouse. One is the spouse who honestly does not think they have anything wrong with them—that they have nothing to confess when it comes to having any major flaws, defects, or issues because they think they are a "really good" person. This is the mindset of the narcissist. When you ask them, "What do you need to change about yourself?" they honestly cannot give you an answer because they do not think there is anything that needs to change.

The other version of the "Nothing to Tell on Myself" spouse is the individual who knows they have issues but is so coated in shame they will not talk about them. They put the "I'm fine" mask on and act as if everything in their life is going great. Anytime their defects peek out from behind the mask, they become anxious that someone might see them for who they really are, bolt the mask down tighter, and keep hiding their flaws.

The "Tell on You" Spouse

This spouse does not confess *their* sins to you, they confess *your* sins to you. This is the spouse who jumps the fence into your backyard and tells you everything that is wrong with you. They do not see any planks in their own eye because they are too busy pointing out all the specks and planks in yours.

In general, we should not tell on others. It is what an elementary school teacher of mine once called being a "tattle tell." Two exceptions to the "do not tell on others" rule are when a person poses a significant threat to themselves or others, or they are engaging in behavior that is significantly damaging to a larger group, organization, or community where you need to be a whistleblower in order to stop what they are doing. Unless these things are going on, I encourage you to stay in your own backyard and own up to all the things wrong with you.

The "False Guilt" Spouse

This spouse confesses wrongdoings to others when they have not actually done anything wrong. These are the spouses who have an overly strict conscience, feel guilty when they have not actually misbehaved (like I feel whenever I see a police car), and apologize when they have nothing to apologize for.

As an example, let's say Sally had emergency surgery, was on life support, and stayed in a coma for three weeks. Then she says to a friend, "Beth, I'm sorry I didn't return your phone call last week. I feel so bad that I didn't." Being on life support and in a coma, Sally could not call Beth, but her overly strict conscience led her to believe she did something wrong. These kinds of people experience a lot of what we call "false guilt" and find themselves apologizing left and right when no apology was necessary.

The "Excuse Making" Spouse

This spouse owns up when they do something wrong, but their apologies have a "but" added to them. When they apologize, it is not really a confession of wrongdoing but an unconscious effort to get others to let them off the hook for the bad stuff they do. It would be like a spouse saying, "I'm sorry I yelled at you the other day and called you a moron, but I have been under a lot of pressure at work and haven't been myself lately." When you add a "but" to a confession of wrongdoing, you are acting as if your wrong behavior was okay or excusable. It was not. Remember, there is never a right reason for wrong behavior.

The "Truly Honest" Spouse

This spouse is doing it right. They admit to having character flaws and defects, own up to the wrong things they have done, and get on the road to recovery. It sounds something like, "Sweetheart, I've been cheating on our taxes for years, the IRS is about to bring the hammer down, and I've kept all of this from you because of how bad I felt about it. Please forgive me for covering this up, especially given that it is going to negatively impact you. I'm truly sorry, and I'm going to get right with the IRS so that there is nothing they need to address with us."

If you are caught up in any of the first four styles, those behaviors are going to get in the way of you and your spouse having a healthy relationship. Keep asking God to help you be the "Truly Honest" spouse so your marriage can be a place of safety and togetherness.

The "Tell on Yourself" Marriage

This might sound a little strange, perhaps even unrealistic, but I believe every married couple needs to have a weekly time where they confess their wrongdoings to each other. I am not suggesting you confess every wrongdoing you commit to your spouse. I think certain things we struggle with are to be confessed to someone else (a trustworthy same-sex friend, colleague, mentor, pastor, or counselor). Using discernment, what I am suggesting is that we get real with our spouse about the struggles we have, so we let them in on the fact we are a real, live human being with issues.

If you agree to do what I am talking about here (set aside fifteen minutes once a week to tell on yourself to your spouse), keep it short and sweet. In other words, do not go into long-winded reasons, much less excuses, for why you struggle the way you do. Simply go right to the specifics of what you did, admit it was wrong, ask for their forgiveness if what you did negatively impacted them, and ask for their support and encouragement to overcome the struggle.

When your spouse confesses their struggles to you, do not try to "fix" them. And, please, do not lecture, shame, or scold them for the struggles they have. Simply offer comfort, encouragement, and understanding. If they ask you for input on it, share your honest feelings about what you think they need to do to overcome their struggles.

One final bit of advice when it comes to the role of confession in marriage. Never remind your spouse of things they did wrong in the past or have already confessed. After they confess to you, do not say, "Sweetie, aren't you forgetting that you lied to me the other day about whether you mailed that package for me like I asked?" Do not tell on your spouse. Ever. You are going to trigger their defensiveness and potentially drive them further into hiding. Trust that God will bring things to your spouse's attention that he wants them to face, will not rub their face in it, and will empower their efforts to make positive changes in their life. It can be a hard thing to face, but God does not need our help when it comes to bringing people under conviction about the things he wants them to address in life.

Perhaps the biggest silver lining to regularly confessing your issues and struggles to your spouse is that it forces you to come out of hiding. It forces you to not sweep your flaws and defects under the marital carpet and hope they go away. And it forces you to keep working on having empathy for how your spouse feels when your actions wound them. The huge upside to healthy confession in marriage is greater compassion toward your mate, increased awareness of the things you need to change, enhanced mutual respect and trust, and greater motivation to get your act together so that you can be a better spouse and human being.

Some Final Thoughts

There are a lot of reasons we do not confess our misdeeds and struggles to our spouse. The single biggest is the shame we feel about what we have done and the struggles we have. Nothing is a more powerful motivator for covering up our struggles than shame.

There are so many positive things waiting for us if we will appropriately confess our sins to our spouse. Confessing our wrongdoings and misdeeds humbles us in that it is an acknowledgment we are imperfect and stand in need of grace and forgiveness from God and those we love here on earth. Confessing our struggles helps us avoid becoming hard-hearted about the wrongs we do and continuing to do them. Confessing our flaws and defects acknowledges our need for people's help to come out of our bondage to destructive ways of living life. Confessing our wrongdoings makes them more concrete and brings their ugliness out of the darkness into the light. Confessing our struggles leads to repairing the damage we have done to our spouse and can lead to healing the relationship. Finally, although it is not guaranteed, confessing our defects can lead to us prospering again in day-to-day life.

You are only as sick as your secrets. With wisdom and discernment, confess your struggles to your spouse, trustworthy others, and God so you can free those relationships to become healthier and more abundant. Commit to a life of no secrets. You will be amazed at how light your life becomes and how much closer you can become to everyone.

CHAPTER ELEVEN

Have Compassion

Nothing helps us build our perspective more than developing compassion for others. Compassion is a sympathetic feeling. It involves the willingness to put yourself in someone else's shoes, to take the focus off yourself and to imagine what it's like to be in someone else's predicament, and simultaneously, to feeling love for that person. It's the recognition that other people's problems, their pain and frustrations, are every bit as real as our own—often far worse. In recognizing this fact and trying to offer some assistance, we open our hearts and greatly enhance our sense of gratitude.

—Richard Carlson

Therefore, as God's chosen people, holy and dearly loved, clothe yourselves with compassion, kindness, humility, gentleness and patience.

—Colossians 3:12

A young minister was about to perform his first wedding ceremony. Fearing he might forget something, he sought counsel from an older preacher. The experienced man told the young minister everything he needed to do and made one final suggestion: "If you ever forget what you are supposed to say, just quote Scripture."

The ceremony went smoothly until the young minister pronounced the happy couple husband and wife. At that point, his mind went blank. That's when he remembered the advice of the old preacher to quote Scripture. So he quoted the only verse that came to his mind: "Father, forgive them, for they know not what they do."

I think we can have compassion for this young minister, don't you? If you have ever been asked to say something at a wedding or other important ceremony, you know how your mind can go blank, and all kinds of inappropriate things can come into your mind and go flying out of your mouth. Yes, I think we can have compassion for this young minister and the pressure he felt to handle his first wedding ceremony well.

It is easy to have compassion for someone when they do something funny that does not wound you, but it is a whole different ball of wax to have compassion when what they have done hurt you in some serious way. If you are like me, compassion in those moments can be hard to come by.

If you want to have a healthy marriage, you need to strengthen the compassion muscle in your soul. Coldhearted, uncompassionate spouses damage the marriage they are in and make it almost impossible for each other to heal from the wounds they inflict on each other. With this in mind, let's return to my counseling office and explore how we can grow in compassion for our spouse so our marriages can be safe and loving places.

The Hard-Hearted Couple

The Bible talks a lot about a hardened heart and how destructive it can be to our relationships with others. This is especially true in marriage. Let's explore two aspects of a hardened heart: First, it could be a heart that has become cold and indifferent. Second, it could be a heart that has become bitter and resentful.

Sadly, Vickie and Ted had both bases covered in their marriage. Over the thirty years they had been married, Vickie had grown cold and indifferent toward Ted, and he had grown resentful and bitter toward her. Vickie did not find Ted interesting or exciting to be around. To put it more bluntly, she found him boring and charmless. Ted, who was not oblivious to the fact that Vickie felt this way, grew more resentful and bitter with each passing year. She increasingly did not want to be around him and preferred the excitement of being with her girlfriends, some of whom were single, and going on trips together where they would party the night away.

They came to see me because they knew their marriage was in trouble. Vickie seemed to understand she had grown cold toward Ted and did not want to be with him anymore. Ted seemed to understand he felt bitter and resentful toward Vickie and that no marriage could last when either person felt the way they did toward each other.

"I know I've grown cold toward Ted, Dr. Thurman, and that it hurts him I feel this way. But I don't know what to do about it. I can't just snap my fingers and magically make it go away," she sighs.

"Well, she's right about it being hurtful. She treats me like she doesn't want to be around me. She'd rather be off with her girlfriends partying than be with me. And I feel bitter about it given that I'm paying for it. She doesn't contribute a dime to our marriage and yet goes off on these expensive trips doing who knows what while she's gone," Ted adds.

"I've told you a thousand times, I don't do anything inappropriate on these trips. My girlfriends who are single are the ones who get all caught up in it and involved with guys they meet," Vickie replies.

"Does it ever occur to you to hang around better people? How good of an influence can they be for you if they're doing that? You're a Christian for crying out loud . . . why don't you start acting like one?" Ted says, going on the attack.

"And stay home and be around you . . . bored out of my mind!" she shoots back.

"I'm not your entertainment. If you want to do something with me, why don't you come up with some ideas?" he asks.

"Why don't you? Why don't you ever plan a date night or a weekend getaway? Why is it all you want to do on the weekends is sit around and watch TV? Do you think that's exciting to me? Of course I find it more enjoyable to be with my girlfriends . . . at least they're not boring!" she answers.

"So, I'm boring, am I?" Ted replies.

"Ted, I know it hurts your feelings, but, yes, I think you're boring. I think left up to you, we would never do anything fun or exciting. When it comes to that part of our marriage, you never lift a finger to make our marriage better. When I see that lack of effort on your part, I become more indifferent . . . even cold. I know we have it in us because, in the past, we had a lot of fun together. As your business grew and once the kids left home, it feels like you've just been mailing it in when it comes to our marriage," Vickie responds.

"Well, since the kids left, it feels like you've become this party animal who's acting like she's single," Ted says with sadness and hurt in his voice.

"That's not what I want. What I want is for you to stop sitting around the house doing nothing but gearing up for another week of work. What I want is a husband who wants to have fun with his wife and do more to pursue her. I'm not asking you to entertain me! I'm just asking you to take more responsibility for making our marriage exciting and enjoyable. Surely we haven't come all this way to end things!" Vickie replies with fear in her voice.

"I think both of you want the same thing . . . a marriage where you enjoy each other's company rather than going through the motions all the time. Sadly, Vickie, it seems you have grown cold and indifferent toward Ted. And, Ted, you seem to have grown resentful and bitter toward Vickie. Neither of you seems to feel much compassion for the other, and that's something I want us to work on in the weeks and months to come," I interject, hoping to encourage them to stay in the marriage and work things out.

"I think you're right," Vicki responds.

"I do, too," Ted adds.

"How about we join together to get the marriage back on track and help you recapture some of the enjoyment you used to feel together?" I ask.

"I'd like that," Vicki replies.

"I would, too," Ted agrees.

The three of us rolled up our sleeves for the next few months. I challenged both of them to have more compassion for where the other was emotionally. I challenged Ted to have more compassion about Vicki's healthy desire to have more fun and excitement in the marriage, and I challenged Vicki to have more compassion about how overwhelmed Ted felt about work and how little energy he had when he came home each night.

Ted began to have more empathy and compassion for how bored Vickie was in the marriage and how hurtful it was that he rarely pursued her or planned for the two of them to do anything fun. Vickie began to have more empathy and compassion for how much pressure Ted was under at work and how exhausted he was when he came home at night. Ted began to assume more responsibility for them having fun together. Vickie backed off going out with girlfriends and was able to be around Ted when he did not have much left in the tank for being fun and exciting.

The bottom line in my work with Vickie and Ted was they had lost compassion for each other. They were not walking in each other's shoes when they first came to see me, leaving one of them feeling cold and indifferent and the other feeling bitter and resentful. Once they started having compassion for what each other's marital world was like, their actions began to change, and a new warmth and tenderness began to emerge.

I wish I could say it always works out this way. Sadly, I have had far too many couples double down on their indifference and coldness and their bitterness and resentment, never letting the other person move back into their heart. That is always a tragedy and something we must never let happen.

When a couple does what Vickie and Ted did, it is a wonderful thing worth celebrating. Compassion heals a lot of wounds in marriage, and I admire any couple willing to put the time and energy into getting there. The more we feel our spouse's pain by walking in their shoes and doing what we can to help them out of it, the healthier and more loving the marriage becomes. It is the way God designed marriage. It is why he tells us to put away all bitterness and rage (Eph. 4:31) and commands us to have compassion for one another (Col. 3:12; 1 Pet. 3:8).

The Eight Aspects of a Hardened Heart in Marriage

A hardened heart has many facets to it. Here, I want to walk you through the eight primary ways a hardened heart can express itself in marriage. All of these are to be avoided at all costs, given how damaging they are to marital health and harmony.

As we go through these, ask yourself if any are descriptive of how you have allowed your heart to atrophy toward your spouse. If any one of the eight describes where you are in your heart toward your spouse, own it and ask God for help to soften your heart.

A Hardened Heart Refuses to Obey

When your heart is hardened toward your spouse, you stop obeying God when it comes to his guidelines for how to interact with your spouse. To put that in the context of this book, you stop complying with the principles we have covered—you refuse to stay in your own backyard, own your own stuff, humble yourself, get your mind right, stop talking trash, shoot straight for their good, wipe the slate clean, and tell on yourself.

A Hardened Heart Does Not Change after Getting Relief from a Painful Circumstance

Even after your spouse has extended forgiveness and grace to you about the hurtful things you have done, a spouse with a hardened heart does not change their hurtful ways. They stiffen their necks, bow their backs, and continue to sin so that grace may abound.

A Hardened Heart Does Not Recognize the Work of God

A spouse with a hardened heart does not recognize God is extending his grace and trying to help them come out of their unhealthy ways of interacting with their partner. They do not see the hand of God on their marriage or their cold and hardened heart toward their spouse. Consequently, they do not appreciate the goodness of God in his efforts to restore their marriage.

A Hardened Heart Is Not Willing to Hear God

A hardened heart leads to not being willing to listen to God. It leads you to shut your ears to the Almighty, and you fall into the dilemma of not having ears to hear the wisdom of God in your marriage (Ezek. 12:2). With no ears to hear, you are left up to your own devices for how you are going to deal with the problems in your marriage. When you are in a troubled marriage, you do not want to listen to yourself; you want to listen to God.

A Hardened Heart Does Not Respect That God Is True to His Word

God promises to help us in time of need (Isa. 40:29, 40:31, 41:10, 41:13). When your heart is hardened, you lose sight of God being a good-hearted promise keeper, and you start to rely on your own power to right the marital ship. As I have said throughout this book, you do not want to turn to your own understanding, insight, and power for how to improve your marriage. God will follow through on his promises to help you if you are in a troubled marriage, but you need to respect that about him rather than question it or doubt it.

A Hardened Heart Remains Hardened Even When the Pain Is Severe

A hardened heart in marriage stays hardened no matter how bad the pain and suffering get. I have seen couples stay hard-hearted toward each other in marriage even though their pain and suffering level went beyond what most of us can handle. Rather than swallow their pride and submit to God's authority, some couples double down on their rebellion against his relationship principles even as their suffering becomes intolerable.

A Hardened Heart May Say the Right Words But Does Not Mean Them

A hard-hearted spouse might say the right words when they mistreat their partner, such as, "I know I'm wrong and need to change," but they do not really mean it. They have what the Bible calls "worldly sorrow [that] brings death" rather than "godly sorrow [that] brings repentance" (2 Cor. 7:10). A hardened heart produces the right words, but it does not lead to the right heartfelt actions. A heart softened by empathy and compassion for one's spouse not only says the right words but means them and lives them out in changed behavior.

A Hardened Heart Does Not Recognize the Turmoil Being Caused

A hardened heart is indifferent to the pain and suffering it causes in the lives of others. A spouse with a hardened heart lacks empathy toward their partner when their own actions cause turmoil and harm in their spouse's life. A properly softened heart feels the pain their spouse experiences when their actions are hurtful.

A Hardened Heart Blames Others Rather Than Themselves for Pain

A spouse with a hardened heart blames their partner for the emotional pain they are in rather than own that a lot of their suffering is self-created. Their heart is too prideful to see that they have met the enemy, and the enemy is them. It is never their fault that they are angry, hurt, or sad—it is always their partner's fault. They are always the victim, never the victimizer.

Not a pretty picture, is it? This is why Scripture says, "Above all else, guard your heart, for everything you do flows from it" (Prov. 4:23). A hardened heart in marriage is a killer. Do everything you can with God's help to keep it soft and malleable.

The "Have Compassion" Marriage

There are a number of practical steps you can take to make your marriage a place of greater compassion. In no particular order, here are seven for you to think about.

Pay Attention

If you are going to have compassion for your spouse, you need to pay attention to their inner world. You need to block out the external and internal distractions in your life and listen deeply to their soul. If you are not fully present and listening at a deep level, your spouse is not going to feel understood, and they are a lot more likely to either grow cold and indifferent or bitter and resentful toward you.

Notice When You Are Being Judgmental

When you listen more deeply to your spouse, it is tempting to be judgmental about what they are saying and who they are as a person. There is a difference between making a judgment about your spouse and being judgmental. You are supposed to judge your spouse's actions ("When you lied to me the other day, that was wrong") but not be judgmental and look down your nose at them ("I would never lie to you! You are a horrible person!"). To have more empathy and compassion, try to avoid being judgmental toward your spouse and limit your judgments to their actions, not their personhood.

Let Go of Being Right

Part of our tendency to be judgmental is tied to our need to be right. If we are going to have compassion for our spouse, we have to let go of the need to be right and simply focus on listening to them as deeply as we can. We table the need to be right in an argument and focus on making sure everyone is being listened to with as much humility and compassion as possible.

Look for Ways to Advocate for Your Spouse

Most of the time, when a spouse expresses they are feeling hurt, they want something from you that is appropriate for them to want. For example, if you have not been paying much attention to your spouse, it is appropriate for them to feel hurt about that and want you to correct things. When your spouse is hurting over not getting what they legitimately need in the marriage, advocate for them. Try to make sure you give them the things they are wired to need in marriage, especially along the lines of meeting their emotional needs (attention, acceptance, appreciation, affirmation, affection, comfort, encouragement, respect, security, support, and understanding).

Do Random Acts of Kindness

Yes, I know. This is a popular bumper sticker. But it is popular for a reason. Do not wait for special occasions to do kind things for your spouse. Surprise them by doing kind things out of the blue so they do not have to wait until a birthday or anniversary to receive these things from you.

Recognize Their Humanness

It is important to walk in your spouse's shoes and realize they are human and that their life is painful and difficult to some degree. Even if you and your spouse have a great life overall, everyone's life is full of challenges and difficulties that are painful. Take time to recognize your spouse's life is hard, and have compassion for the fact they are doing the best they can to deal with the day-to-day problems that come their way.

Understand Their Side of the Story

Far too often, when couples talk about difficult things, each person is focused on being understood and not on being understanding. Whether you agree with what they say or not, listen carefully enough to understand their thoughts and feelings about a particular issue or situation. Do not seek to be understood until you seek to understand.

Some Final Thoughts

Far too many people carry a lack of compassion for their spouse into marriage each day. More often than not, it is a self-protective mechanism for how we cope with feeling our spouse does not have much compassion for us ("Well, if they are not going to have any compassion for me, I'm not going to have any for them!"). The bill comes due sooner or later because relationships cannot be loving if compassion is not running the show.

No relationship can survive either person lacking compassion for the other's pain, and it is not uncommon for people to go their separate ways when this is the case. This is why when I am working with couples, I always have them write two essays. One is, "How have I hurt my spouse and how did they feel?" and "How has my spouse hurt me and how did I feel?" Here, I am not trying to rub anyone's nose in how hurtful they have been as a spouse. I just want them to face it and develop greater empathy and compassion toward themselves and their spouse that they have wounded each other.

According to the Bible, if we lack love and compassion for others, we are like a clanging cymbal or a resounding gong (1 Cor. 13:1). I say this simply to light a fire underneath us so we will work harder in this crucial area of life. Whether we were the one who hurt our spouse or they were the one who hurt us, we need to have compassion for how everyone feels in the midst of these painful relationship ruptures.

Above all else, guard your heart. With God's help, make sure your heart never grows cold and indifferent or bitter and resentful toward your spouse. Make sure you walk in your spouse's shoes each day to experience what they feel as they go through life, especially the life you have together as a couple. Compassion goes a long way in healing marital wounds and can help the two of you grow closer than you ever thought possible.

PART THREE

SAVING YOUR MARRIAGE BEFORE IT FAILS

CHAPTER TWELVE

Persevere through Thick and Thin, Especially the Thin

By perseverance the snail reached the ark.

—Charles Spurgeon

Let perseverance finish its work so that you may be mature and complete, not lacking anything.

—James 1:4

A husband and wife had been married for sixty years and had no secrets except for one: The woman kept in her closet a shoe box that she forbade her husband from ever opening. But when she was on her deathbed—and with her blessing—he opened the box and found a crocheted doll and $95,000 in cash.

"My mother told me that the secret to a happy marriage was to never argue," she explained. "Instead, I should keep quiet and crochet a doll."

Her husband was touched. Only one doll was in the box—that meant she'd been angry with him only once in sixty years. "But what about all this money?" he asked.

"Oh," she said. "That's the money I made from selling the dolls."

Having a healthy, flourishing marriage is difficult because to do it we have to honestly face ourselves. We have to honestly face the fact that we are fallen human beings who have a hard time complying with the relationship principles we have covered in this book. Consequently, we do not treat our spouse in the kind, compassionate, and loving manner we are supposed to.

Far too many of us think marriage should be easy and require very little effort. We think that after falling head over heels in love with our future spouse, we are going to be on Easy Street and getting along will be a breeze. Refusing to accept the truth that marriage is both complex and difficult can lead to bailing out when the going gets tough (which it always does).

In light of the fact that co-creating a healthy, thriving marriage is difficult, I have a question for all of us. Are we going to keep taking the easier path of showing up in marriage expecting it to go well on its own and pulling away when it is hard, or are we going to take the less-traveled path of living by the principles we have covered in this book to ensure our marriage will go well? The choice is ours, and it is a choice we face every single day.

These principles for a healthy marriage were laid down a long time ago by the God who said, "It is not good for the man to be alone" (Gen. 2:18). We either humbly submit to them no matter how hard it is, or we reject them as if they apply to everyone else but us. We do not get to choose the principles for the actions it takes to get along well with our spouse, but we do get to choose whether or not we live by them.

Prewired into the choice we make on following these principles or rejecting them is a guaranteed outcome. If we follow these principles and the person we are married to does as well, we will get along well with each other and experience a deeper closeness over time. If we refuse to follow these rules, we will not get along with our spouse, and deeper levels of conflict, woundedness, and emotional pain are going to damage the marriage.

People who read a book like this are usually the ones willing to make their marriage better. If you have reached this point in the book, I am guessing you are that kind of person—someone willing to do what it takes to get along better with your spouse and prayerfully hoping your spouse will do the same. I applaud your willingness to do the hard work of developing a loving bond with your spouse, and I pray your spouse will return the favor.

I recently laid some sod in my yard, and the grass company that sold it to me made it clear I needed to water it heavily in the first month of putting it in. They made it clear that the sod would not take root and grow if I did not follow their instructions. I want you to think that way about the ten principles of marriage we have covered—you and your spouse need to water these principles into your marriage, not just for the next thirty days but for the rest of your marriage, so that they deeply take root and help you experience a thriving relationship.

With that in mind, let me walk you back through the ten principles we have covered for having a close relationship.

Let's Review, Shall We?

When I was a first-time college professor, those who had been teaching for a while would say, "Chris, tell your students what you are going to tell them, tell it to them, and then tell them what you told them." I told you in the first chapter what I was going to tell you in this book, and I used the next ten chapters to tell it to you. Now I would like to tell you what I told you about how to have a loving, intimate relationship with your spouse.

Stay in Your Own Backyard

We have a tendency to focus on our spouse's flaws rather than our own. To get along well in marriage, we have to focus on our own flaws and defects, not on our spouse's. We have to be willing to take the plank out of our own eye before we try to remove the specks (or planks) from our spouse's eye (Luke 6:42). If we focus on our spouse's flaws, our marriage cannot be the healthy, loving, and safe place God wants it to be.

Own Your Own Stuff

We tend to blame our feelings and actions on our spouse, especially when they were the one who triggered them. Not only do we need to focus on our own flaws in marriage, but we need to make sure we do not blame them on our spouse. We need to take full responsibility for what we feel and how we act in marriage, not blame either on our partner. A marriage cannot be the loving, safe place God wants it to be if we blame our "stuff" on our spouse.

Give More Than You Take

All of us struggle with a tendency to take rather than give. To have a flourishing marriage, we have to be in "give" mode, not "take" mode. We have to meet our spouse's needs first, put our needs on the back burner, and trust our spouse will return the favor. We need to be open to our spouse meeting our needs, but we need to try to meet their needs before they meet ours, as often as possible. Each day, we want the marital ledger to read we gave as much, if not more, than we received.

Humble Yourself

We are prone to be a little too full of ourselves at times. To get along well with our spouse, we have to humble ourselves, thinking neither more highly nor more lowly of ourselves than we should. We have to reject inaccurate positive or negative views of ourselves, views that do not square up with who we really are. We have to resist the urge to make our good qualities better than they are and our bad qualities worse than they are. Grandiosity, pride, and arrogance have to be put away in a loving marriage, and humility of spirit has to run the show.

Get Your Mind Right

All of us struggle with some degree of "stinking thinking" when it comes to false beliefs about marriage. For a marriage to thrive, we have to view reality accurately, believe what is true, and reject false notions about interpersonal relationships. "Garbage in, garbage out" is a principle that applies to all aspects of life, but it is especially true in marriage. Faulty beliefs, attitudes, and expectations make it impossible to successfully repair relational wounds and experience a healthy, loving closeness with each other.

Stop Talking Trash

It is a hard thing to admit, but we sometimes fall into being verbally abusive in marriage. To thrive, we have to stop "talking trash" to our spouse. We have to stop criticizing our spouse, trivializing their wants and needs, blaming them for things they are not responsible for, threatening them with dire consequences if we do not get our way, calling them names, manipulating them to get what we want, and yelling at them, just to name a few of the ways we are verbally abusive. We have to say words that are wholesome and build our spouse up, not words that denigrate or demean them.

Shoot Straight for Their Good

We have a tendency to give our spouse inaccurate feedback out of an unhealthy desire to hurt them for how they have wounded us. A thriving marriage requires that we are honest with each other about things that are hurtful. It also requires that we say what we do out of a desire to facilitate our spouse's growth, not out of a desire to demean or denigrate them. True marital friends speak the truth in love to each other so the marriage can be a healthy one.

Wipe the Slate Clean

It can be hard to forgive our spouse when they hurt us, especially if the wound was a deep one and we feel they either do not care or will not take responsibility for hurting us. To experience a loving marriage, we have to forgive our spouse when they mistreat us. We have to wipe the debt of their mistreatment off the marital books, start with a zero balance each day, and work hard to avoid falling back into bitterness and unforgiveness again. We have to face the fact we are as fallen as they are, have done just as much to hurt them as they have us, and stand in need of just as much forgiveness as they do. While our spouse is being hurtful, we need to have healthy, firm boundaries if they will not stop. God wants us to forgive our spouse for the hurtful things they do, but he does not want us to tolerate or enable sinful mistreatment.

Tell on Yourself

We are only as sick as our secrets. A safe, loving marriage requires that we confess our misdeeds and struggles to each other and let our spouse in on what is really going on in our life. We have to be willing to "get real," take our mask off, and join the rest of the human race as a deeply flawed person struggling to get his or her act together. We have to be discerning about what we share with our spouse and take certain struggles to wise, trustworthy, same-sex people for input and accountability to overcome a struggle.

Have Compassion

A hard-hearted marriage, whether it takes the form of being cold and indifferent toward our spouse or bitter and resentful, is a dead marriage. Every couple can fall into having a hardened heart toward each other. Through trying to better understand our spouse and have more compassion for how hard their life is, we can soften our heart toward them and bring the marriage back to life. It is especially hard to have empathy and compassion toward our spouse when what they do wounds us, but that is the example Christ sets for us. He was deeply wounded by many of the people around him, but he always had compassion for how lost they were. We need to do the same toward our spouse so that we do not fall into either a cold or an embittered heart.

These principles are all marital lifesavers because they challenge us to grow into more mature, loving people. Their application demands we leave our childish, immature ways behind us (1 Cor. 13:11) and become full-fledged adults. However difficult these principles are to live by, they are well worth it because of the wonderful results they produce in marriage.

Let me give you another very important reason to live by these principles: Doing so gives your children a better picture of what a mature and loving marriage looks like so they can aspire to reproduce it in their own marriages later on. The generational drift of toxic, unhealthy marriages can be turned around if we commit to following these principles and give our children a whole new vision for what marriage can look like when it is done right.

The Persevering Marriage

Given how complex and difficult marriage is, it can be easy to get discouraged, throw in the towel, and walk away. Marriage is not for the faint of heart, and it is not for quitters either. While I do believe there are times a marriage is damaged beyond repair, either because the offending spouse will not stop acting badly or the offended spouse will not forgive, I believe the vast majority of marriages can be saved before they fail. But to save a marriage before it fails, you have to have something called perseverance.

Perseverance is not doing the same thing over and over again and expecting a different result. That's insanity, not perseverance. Perseverance is doing the right thing over and over again, no matter how hard it is, something that leads to better results over time.

I have turned the word perseverance into an acronym, PERSEVERANCE, to walk you through the key characteristics of this crucial aspect of a healthy marriage. For your consideration, here are the twelve core aspects of perseverance.

Patience: We have to be patient and allow growth in marriage to play out over time.

Endurance: We have to bear the pain we experience in our efforts to have a thriving marriage.

Resilience: We have to bounce back up when we experience a marital setback.

Sacrifice: We have to sacrifice time, energy, and resources to achieve a healthy, loving marriage.

Effort: We have to give our full effort in marriage each day, avoiding lethargy and laziness.

Vision: We have to have a clear vision of what we are trying to accomplish in marriage. Without a vision for where we are headed, it is harder to stay the course.

Experience: We have to execute our plan and learn from the mistakes we make along the way.

Relationships: We need to involve others in our efforts to achieve a thriving marriage, not leave people out and try to do things Lone Ranger style.

Attitude: We have to have a realistic and an optimistic attitude in pursuing our marital aspirations.

Necessity: We need to do whatever it takes, within biblical and moral constraints, to achieve our marital goals.

Courage: We need to avoid giving in to a spirit of fear in marriage and courageously press on when we run into a setback or roadblock.

Enthusiasm: We need to be energetic and passionate about our marital goals and not allow indifference to come into play.

These twelve aspects of perseverance are crucial if we are going to finish the marital race well and claim the prize of greater closeness, compassion, and friendship. Failure to do even just one of these can get in the way of having a successful, thriving marriage. All of them together can take your marriage to places you never thought possible.

We live in a time when a lot of couples bail on marriage. They find it too hard and lose the will to carry on, especially when they feel their spouse refuses to join them in the effort to make the marriage better. The divorce rate and high number of unhappy marriages reflect many things, but they certainly reflect that perseverance is a hard thing to come by in many relationships.

I want to encourage you to persevere in your marriage and make a commitment to each other to abide by the ten principles of marriage we've covered in this book the rest of your days on earth. It will be hard, but you will not regret it. God has some wonderful things waiting on you if you will take the wise path of adhering to his principles rather than continuing to live by your own. You will be eternally glad you did.

Some Final Thoughts

I traveled to Israel a number of years ago and saw things that made my jaw drop. One place I found especially interesting was the pool at Bethesda where Christ encountered a man who had been an invalid for thirty-eight years. The pool at Bethesda was rumored to have healing powers when stirred, and this man had been unable to get himself in the waters fast enough to experience the healing that was supposed to take place. Jesus entered the scene and chose this one man out of the crowd to heal.

Knowing this man might have grown accustomed to being an invalid (thirty-eight years is a long time to hope for healing), Christ asked him a question that reverberates through history: "Do you want to get well?" (John 5:6). That was either an incredibly insulting question or an incredibly insightful one. I often ask it of the couples who come to see me. I ask it because I am concerned that they have so completely adjusted to being unhappy and at odds with each other that they no longer want to do what it takes to turn things around.

That is the question I want to ask you before I close this book. Do you want to get well when it comes to your marriage? Are you ready, willing, and able to do whatever it takes for as long as it takes to develop a loving, tender, kind, and compassionate relationship with your spouse? Are you willing to drop your pride at the doorstep of your home each day and humbly submit to God's principles for thriving with your spouse?

That is my hope for those of us who are married. Even though the spiritual, psychological, and cultural forces that oppose marriage are strong, we serve a God who is so much stronger. We serve a God who promised "that he who began a good work in you will carry it on to completion until the day of Christ Jesus" (Phil. 1:6). Let's rest on the promise that God, having begun a good work in us in marriage, will carry it on to completion. Let's rest on the promise that God will persevere alongside us in the years to come, to help us develop a close marital bond that will be worth every ounce of blood, sweat, and tears we experience along the way.

I will be praying for you to that end.

REAL MARRIAGE MADE SIMPLE WORKBOOK

DR. CHRIS THURMAN

LESSON ONE

Can't We Just Get Along?

In this first lesson, I want you to take time to assess where you are when it comes to the ten principles of marriage covered in this book.

Complete the self-assessment inventory using the scale below. Be honest about how you *actually* think and avoid responding with how you *should* think. Also, try to avoid using the neutral response (5/6).

1 2 3 4 5 6 7 8 9 10

Strongly Disagree Neutral Strongly Agree

_______ 1. I focus on my spouse's flaws and defects rather than my own.

_______ 2. I blame my feelings and actions on my spouse.

_______ 3. I take more than I give in marriage.

_______ 4. I am not humble in my marriage.

_______ 5. I have many faulty beliefs, attitudes, and expectations about marriage.

_______ 6. I talk a lot of trash to my spouse.

_______ 7. I am not accurate or loving in what I say to my spouse.

_______ 8. I struggle to forgive my spouse when they hurt me.

_______ 9. I do not share my flaws and defects with my spouse.

_______ 10. My heart is hardened toward my spouse.

Add all your responses and divide by ten. This is the average degree to which you agree with these statements. Next, look through your answers and circle the statements you gave an eight, nine, or ten. These responses suggest you hold more strongly to these *unhealthy* ways of interacting with your spouse.

Next, I want you to give examples of where you fall into not being emotionally healthy in the ten ways listed above. Try to be as specific as you can concerning what thoughts, feelings, and actions you have in each area. And remember, do not condemn or put yourself down for acting in these ways—just allow God to help you come under conviction and head in a better direction.

I focus on my spouse's flaws and defects in the following ways:

I blame my spouse for my feelings and actions in the following ways:

I take more than I give to my spouse in the following ways:

I am not humble toward my spouse in the following ways:

My mind isn't right about marriage in the following ways:

I talk trash to my spouse in the following ways:

I talk inaccurately about and unlovingly toward my spouse in the following ways:

I withhold forgiveness from my spouse in the following ways:

I am not honest or transparent with my spouse about the following struggles in my life:

____

____

____

____

____

I am hard-hearted (cold/indifferent and/or bitter/resentful) toward my spouse in the following ways:

____

____

____

____

____

The purpose of this assignment is not to rub your face in how you treat your spouse. It is simply to help you be honest about how you interact with them. We all struggle to live according to God's principles for healthy relationships. The first step in creating a more loving marriage is to be honest about it and commit to taking a new path.

If you want to learn more about developing a healthier, more loving marriage with your spouse, please consider the following resources.

Recommended Reading

Boundaries in Marriage: Understanding the Choices That Make or Break Loving Relationships by Henry Cloud and John Townsend

How We Love: Discover Your Love Style, Enhance Your Marriage by Milan and Kay Yerkovich

Sacred Marriage: What If God Designed Marriage to Make Us Holy More Than to Make Us Happy? by Gary Thomas

Saving Your Marriage Before It Starts: Seven Questions to Ask Before—and After—You Marry by Les and Leslie Parrott

The 5 Love Languages: The Secret to Love That Lasts by Gary Chapman

The Meaning of Marriage: Facing the Complexities of Commitment with the Wisdom of God by Timothy Keller and Kathy Keller

LESSON TWO

Staying in Your Own Backyard

In many marriages, there is a tendency to focus on the flaws and defects in our spouse rather than focusing on our own. It is one of the many ways we run from the fact that we are imperfect human beings, and it contributes to marriage not being a safe place for our spouse to face their own flaws and grow into a healthier, more loving human being.

More often than not, we focus on our spouse's flaws because we carry around shame about our own. By focusing on our spouse's defects, we unhealthily run from how bad we feel about the ones we have. This gets in the way of honestly facing our own fallenness and growing into a more mature, loving adult.

As you work through this lesson, take time to think about the flaws and defects you tend to focus on about your spouse. Then consider your own flaws and defects. Notice that you may be avoiding key truths about yourself as you focus on your spouse's shortcomings.

The Flaws and Defects of My Spouse

When you find yourself looking over the fence into your spouse's backyard, what are the flaws you tend to focus on?

Spouse Flaw #1:

Spouse Flaw #2:

Spouse Flaw #3:

The Personal Flaws I'm Running From

When you focus on your spouse's flaws, you are usually running from your own. When you are peering over the fence looking at the defects in your spouse, what defects about yourself are you running from?

Personal Flaw #1:

Personal Flaw #2:

Personal Flaw #3:

How I Respond to My Spouse When I Am Focused on Their Flaws

How do you treat your spouse when you are focused on their issues rather than your own?

How I Respond to My Spouse When I Am Focused on My Own Flaws

Write down how you treat your spouse when you focus on your own issues rather than theirs.

What Things Bother You about Your Spouse That You Struggle With?

Fairly often, the things that bother us about others are things we struggle with ourselves. In the space below, write down what bothers you about your spouse that you struggle with yourself.

Example #1:

Example #2:

Example #3:

If we are going to have a healthy marriage, we must spend the majority of our time in our own backyard focusing on the flaws and defects we brought into the marriage. We must avoid looking over the fence into our spouse's backyard, much less jump the fence and camp out in their flaws and defects. We must humble ourselves and let God use our marriage to help us face our own issues and grow into a more loving, mature spouse.

Read Galatians 6:7–10

What feelings and thoughts come to mind as you consider this passage?

How does this passage apply to marriage?

If you want to do a better job of staying in your own backyard, please consider reading the books listed below.

Recommended Reading

Blind Spots: Why We Fail to Do What's Right and What to Do about It by Max Bazerman and Ann Tenbrunsel

Looking in the Mirror: Daily Quotes for Self-Examination and Critical Thinking by R. Alvin Jones

Making Judgments without Being Judgmental: Nurturing a Clear Mind and a Generous Heart by Terry D. Cooper

The Necessity of Self-Examination by Jonathan Edwards

Who Are You to Judge? The Dangers of Judging and Legalism by Dave Swavely

LESSON THREE

Owning Your Own Stuff

At times, we fall into not taking appropriate responsibility in our interactions with our spouse. One mistake we make is to take too much responsibility, which leads to feeling responsible for their feelings and actions. We referred to this as being neurotic in marriage. The other mistake we make is to take too little responsibility, which leads to blaming our feelings and actions on them. We referred to this as being character disordered in marriage. Whether we take too much responsibility or not enough, both are damaging to our own emotional health and the health of our relationship with our spouse.

First, I want you to write down a couple of examples where you take too much responsibility (being neurotic) in your marriage. Here, try to recall situations where you felt responsible for your spouse's feelings, thoughts, and actions.

I take too much responsibility for my spouse when I:

I take too much responsibility for my spouse when I:

Next, I want you to write down a couple of examples where you take too little responsibility (being character disordered) in your marriage. Here, try to recall situations where you blamed your spouse for your feelings, thoughts, and actions.

I took too little responsibility when I blamed my spouse for:

I took too little responsibility when I blamed my spouse for:

In each of the situations you described, I want you to write down what you were responsible for and what your spouse was responsible for.

Regarding the first situation where I took *too much* responsibility, I was responsible for . . .

and my spouse was responsible for . . .

Regarding the second situation where I took *too much* responsibility, I was responsible for . . .

and my spouse was responsible for . . .

Regarding the first situation where I took *too little* responsibility, I was responsible for . . .

and my spouse was responsible for . . .

Regarding the second situation where I took *too little* responsibility, I was responsible for . . .

and my spouse was responsible for . . .

Keep a Marital Responsibility Journal for a Week

I do not like to journal any more than the next guy or gal, but when I take the time to do it, it always leaves me more aware of how I think, feel, and act from day to day.

In the space provided below, I want you to write about two things that happen in your marriage this week. First, write about situations where you blamed your feelings and actions on your spouse. Second, write about situations where you felt responsible for your spouse's feelings and actions.

I blamed my spouse for my feelings and actions when . . .

I felt responsible for my spouse's feelings and actions when . . .

To have healthier marriages, we must take complete responsibility for our own feelings and actions while holding our spouse to the same standard. We cannot afford to take too much responsibility in marriage (neurotic), nor too little (character disordered). Either mistake ensures we will not get along as well as we could in our day-to-day interactions.

Do your marriage a favor. Own your own stuff and encourage your spouse to do the same. You will be surprised by how much your marriage will grow and mature.

If you want to get better at owning your own stuff in marriage, please consider reading the books listed the on next page.

Recommended Reading

Boundaries: When to Say Yes, How to Say No to Take Control of Your Life by Henry Cloud and John Townsend

Boundaries in Marriage: Understanding the Choices That Make or Break Loving Relationships by Henry Cloud and John Townsend

But It's Not My Fault (Responsible Me!) by Julia Cook and Anita DuFalla

Stepping Up: How Taking Responsibility Changes Everything by John Izzo

The Berenstain Bears and the Blame Game by Stan and Jan Berenstain

The Road Less Traveled: A New Psychology of Love, Traditional Values and Spiritual Growth by M. Scott Peck

LESSON FOUR

Giving More Than You Take

While there are many ways to give more than you take in marriage, I emphasize giving to your spouse by meeting their psychological needs (attention, acceptance, appreciation, affirmation, affection, comfort, encouragement, respect, support, security, and understanding). In light of this list, I want you to do some honest self-examination (not self-condemnation) along the lines of how well or poorly you meet the psychological needs of your spouse. Take a "thirty-thousand foot" view of how good or bad you have been at meeting these needs.

When it comes to giving my spouse attention, I:

When it comes to accepting my spouse "warts and all," I:

When it comes to giving my spouse nonsexual affection, I:

When it comes to affirming my spouse's positive character qualities, I:

When it comes to appreciating my spouse's positive actions, I:

When it comes to giving my spouse comfort when they're sad, I:

When it comes to encouraging my spouse when they're discouraged, I:

When it comes to showing my spouse respect in how I treat them, I:

When it comes to my spouse feeling secure in our relationship (that I am not going to abandon or reject them), I:

When it comes to giving my spouse support through acts of service, I:

When it comes to being understanding of how my spouse thinks and feels about things, I:

Now, I want you to be more specific. Across each of the eleven psychological needs we have listed, I want you to write down how you are going to do a better job of meeting these needs in your spouse.

I am going to be more accepting of my spouse by:

I am going to be more affectionate toward my spouse by:

I am going to be more affirming of my spouse's positive character qualities by:

____

____

____

____

____

I am going to be more appreciative toward my spouse by:

____

____

____

____

____

I am going to be more attentive toward my spouse by:

____

____

____

____

____

I am going to give my spouse more comfort when they are sad by:

I am going to be more encouraging toward my spouse by:

I am going to show more respect toward my spouse by:

I am going to provide more emotional security for my spouse by:

____

____

____

____

____

I am going to be more supportive (acts of service) of my spouse by:

____

____

____

____

____

I am going to be more understanding of my spouse by:

____

____

____

____

____

If you want to have a better marriage, you must make sure you spend each day meeting these psychological needs in your spouse and trust they will return the favor. Even if your spouse does not return the favor, this is how we are to love them in a sacrificial manner that brings glory to God.

If you want to get better at giving more than you take in marriage, please consider reading the books listed below.

Recommended Reading

Developing a Servant's Heart: Become Fully Like Christ by Serving Others by Charles Stanley

Full Service: Moving from Self-Serve Christianity to Full Servanthood by Siang-Yang Tan

Hold Me Tight: Seven Conversations for a Lifetime of Love by Sue Johnson

How We Love: Discover Your Love Style, Enhance Your Marriage by Milan and Kay Yerkovich

Humility: The Journey toward Holiness by Andrew Murray

Leaders Eat Last: Why Some Teams Pull Together and Others Don't by Simon Sinek

On Being a Servant of God by Warren Wiersbe

The Giving Tree by Shel Silverstein

LESSON FIVE

Humbling Yourself

There are numerous ways to humble yourself in marriage. Let me give you my "Sixteen Ways to Practice Humility in Marriage" list for your consideration.

Sixteen Ways to Practice Humility in Marriage

With each entry, write a thought or two about specific ways you can practice this aspect of humility in your marriage.

Ask Your Spouse for Feedback

Very few things will humble you faster than asking your spouse to give you both positive and negative feedback on your behavior.

Give Credit for Your Spouse's Ideas, Especially When You Benefitted from Them

Practice humility by "giving credit where credit is due."

Admit When You Are Wrong about Something You Said or Did

Humble yourself by acknowledging when you expressed an incorrect view or opinion or did an incorrect action.

Admit When You Do Not Know or Understand Something Very Well

Be humble enough to admit when you do not know very much about a given topic or area of life.

Acknowledge Your Spouse's Superior Talents and Abilities

Try not to be threatened by the fact that your spouse is more talented or gifted than you at certain things.

Apologize to Your Spouse When You Do Something Selfish or Immature

We all act selfishly and immaturely at times and need to apologize and ask our spouse to forgive us when we do.

Study Biblical Character Development and Morality with Your Spouse

Humble yourself by studying the perfect moral righteousness of God and the ways he dealt with the character defects and flaws of major figures in the Bible.

Acknowledge That Your Gifts, Talents, and Abilities Are from God

Give God the credit for the positive things you bring to the marriage.

Acknowledge Your Talents, Skills, and Abilities Have Been Developed with the Help of Your Spouse, Others, and God

You did not get better by yourself. Take time to acknowledge the people who helped you grow into a more mature and loving person.

Pay Your Talents, Abilities, and Skills Forward to Your Spouse

Do not keep your positive qualities and abilities to yourself. Pass them along to your spouse to help them improve as well, even if it means they surpass you.

Remember, Compared to God, You Are No Better or Worse Than Your Spouse

Avoid looking down your nose at your spouse. Remember that compared to Christ, you are fundamentally no different from any other human being.

Let Your Spouse Go First

Look out for your spouse by letting them go ahead of you when possible. You might hold a door open for them and let them go through it first, let them go through the lunch line first, or let them be the first to speak when you are around others.

Do Not Assume Anything about Your Spouse

Get to know your spouse more deeply before you make any assumptions or judgments about why they act the way they do.

Practice an Act of Humility toward Your Spouse Each Day

Do not let a day go by without serving your spouse in a humble manner. Ask if you can bring them something from the kitchen; ask if you can do something for them around the house that is their job to do; offer to go get something they need from the grocery store rather than make them go get it themselves.

Stay in Learning Mode about Your Spouse

We never master anything in life, especially knowing our spouse fully, and we need to constantly be "in the classroom" learning more about them along the way.

Talk about Yourself as Little as Possible

Put your focus on letting your spouse talk about himself or herself, and avoid bringing the focus back to you.

There are dozens of other ways to practice humility in marriage. Please consider practicing the ones listed above each day.

If you want to get better at humbling yourself in marriage, please consider reading the books listed below.

Recommended Reading

Humility: The Journey toward Holiness by Andrew Murray
Humility: The Forgotten Virtue by Wayne Mack
Humility: True Greatness by C. J. Mahaney
The Blessing of Humility by Jerry Bridges
The Freedom of Self-Forgetfulness: The Path to True Christian Joy by Timothy Keller
Humble Roots: How Humility Grounds and Nourishes Your Soul by Hannah Anderson

LESSON SIX

Getting Your Mind Right

To get along better with your spouse, you must dedicate your mind to seeing things accurately and realistically. Faulty ways of viewing reality harm you and your spouse, whereas reality-based ways of thinking help you thrive as a couple. The truth, when deeply believed, sets you free to enjoy greater levels of emotional and relational health. Lies, when deeply believed, make your life an emotional and interpersonal mess.

Do some self-assessment of the beliefs you have about marriage. Assess your beliefs using the self-assessment inventory below. Be honest about how you *actually* think and avoid responding in terms of how you *should* think. Also, try to avoid using the neutral response (5/6). Take time to consider each statement and answer honestly to how much you agree or disagree with what it says.

1 2 3 4 5 6 7 8 9 10

Strongly Disagree — Neutral — Strongly Agree

_______ 1. The purpose of marriage is to make me happy.
_______ 2. My spouse can completely meet all my emotional needs.
_______ 3. My spouse is a bigger mess of a human being than I am.

_______ 4. I am entitled to my spouse's love and respect.
_______ 5. Our marital problems are all my spouse's fault.
_______ 6. My spouse should accept me as I am.
_______ 7. My spouse should be just like me.
_______ 8. I see my spouse for who they really are.
_______ 9. My spouse must earn my forgiveness.
_______ 10. My spouse and I can reconcile without either of us changing our ways.

Add all your answers up and divide by ten. This is the average degree to which you believe these statements, all of which (I believe) are false. Next, go back through the questionnaire and circle any statement you gave an eight, nine, or ten. These (I believe) are your strongest false beliefs about marriage and the ones causing you and your spouse the most harm.

Take the statements you believed the most strongly and write down the truth that would counter the false belief. Do not argue with the false belief in doing this assignment; just write down what the truth, as best you can determine it, happens to be.

False Belief I Hold Strongly: ______________________________

____

Truth about This False Belief: ______________________________

____

____

False Belief I Hold Strongly: ______________________________

____

Truth about This False Belief: ______________________________

False Belief I Hold Strongly:

Truth about This False Belief:

Before we finish this lesson, I want you to do some additional work on the lie of entitlement in marriage. As hard as it is to accept this, we are not entitled to *anything* in marriage. We are not entitled to our spouse's affirmation, respect, support, appreciation, or any of the other psychological needs we carry around inside of us. To put it broadly, we are not entitled to our spouse's love.

In the space provided below, write down what you find yourself feeling entitled to in marriage.

In my marriage, I am entitled to:

In my marriage, I am entitled to:

In my marriage, I am entitled to:

Now I want you to take each issue you feel entitled to in marriage and restate it as a valid want or desire.

In my marriage, it is legitimate to want:

In my marriage, it is legitimate to want:

In my marriage, it is legitimate to want:

Finally, I want you to write a brief essay about why you are not entitled to anything in marriage but why it is legitimate to want your valid needs met by your spouse.

The truth will set us free, but we have to work hard to internalize it in the deepest recesses of our mind. Erroneous beliefs we learned in childhood, especially about relationships, may have made sense to us back then, but they cannot help us function as mature adults in the here and now. With God's help, keep working on renewing your mind in marriage so you can experience the emotional, relational, and spiritual health available to you in life.

If you want to get your mind right in marriage, please consider reading the books listed below.

Recommended Reading

Get Out of Your Mind and Into Your Life: The New Acceptance and Commitment Therapy by Steven Hayes with Spencer Smith

The Lies Couples Believe: How Living the Truth Transforms Your Marriage by Chris Thurman

The Lies We Believe (30th Anniversary Edition): Renew Your Mind and Transform Your Life by Chris Thurman

The Lies We Believe about God: Knowing God for Who He Really Is by Chris Thurman

Winning the War in Your Mind: Change Your Thinking, Change Your Life by Craig Groeschel

LESSON SEVEN

Stopping Talking Trash

The words we say matter because they have the power to build our spouse up or tear them down. Not only do we need to be more careful when it comes to what we say, we need to be more careful when it comes to how we say it.

Evaluating the Language Used in Your Marriage

Looking back in time, what are some of the worst things you have said to your spouse, words that tore them down and demeaned them?

On the flip side, what are the kindest things you have said to your spouse, words that built them up and left them encouraged?

What are some of the most hurtful things your spouse has said to you?

What are some of the kindest things your spouse has said to you?

We covered numerous aspects of verbal abuse in marriage. Without beating yourself up about it, write down specific ways you have fallen into these abusive styles of interacting with your spouse.

Discounting

Denying that your spouse has a right to their thoughts or feelings and telling them they are being too sensitive, emotional, or childish.

Biting Humor

Using humor to put your spouse down.

Blaming

Holding your spouse responsible for things that are outside their control or sphere of influence.

Judging

Negatively evaluating your spouse and putting them down in the process.

Trivializing

Making the things your spouse does or wants seem small and insignificant.

Threatening

Making explicit threats about what you are going to do if your spouse does not do what you want.

Name-Calling

Calling your spouse derogatory names.

Denying and Rationalizing

Refusing to acknowledge your bad behavior or attempting to justify it.

Being Tonal

Using the tone of your voice to put your spouse down.

Manipulating

Using words to manipulate your spouse into giving you what you want.

Not Taking Responsibility

Not owning your feelings or actions but instead blaming them on your spouse.

Making Accusations

Repetitively accusing your spouse of something because of your own insecurities or arrogance.

Being Bossy

Frequently telling your spouse what to do.

Being Condescending

Looking down your nose at your spouse because you think you are better than them.

____

____

____

____

____

We all know that words matter and matter a lot. Keep working on eliminating the bad ones and saying more of the good ones toward your spouse. With God's help, do the best you can to comply with the biblical challenge: "Do not let any unwholesome talk come out of your mouths, but only what is helpful for building others up according to their needs, that it may benefit those who listen" (Eph. 4:29).

If you want to get better at speaking to your spouse in ways that build them up and encourage them, please consider reading the books listed below.

Recommended Reading

Keep It Shut: What to Say, How to Say It, and When to Say Nothing at All by Karen Ehman

The Emotionally Destructive Marriage: How to Find Your Voice and Reclaim Your Hope by Leslie Vernick

The Verbally Abusive Relationship: How to Recognize It and How to Respond by Patricia Evans

Watch Your Mouth: Understanding the Power of the Tongue by Tony Evans

Watch Your Mouth Interactive Workbook: Understanding the Power of the Tongue by Tony Evans

LESSON EIGHT

Shooting Straight for Their Good

If you are going to "speak the truth in love" (Eph. 4:15 NLT) to your spouse, you must learn to listen more deeply and attentively to the things they say. Learning to listen deeply to your spouse is one of the most important ways you can become closer to each other and get along better. In this lesson, I am going to take you into the most important listening skills you can develop and ask you to work on them with your spouse.

Fifteen Ways to Become a Better Listener in Marriage

Following are fifteen ways to become a better listener when interacting with your spouse. Each of the communication skills paves the way for you to speak the truth in love to each other at a much higher level. In the spaces provided, express how you stack up in each area when it comes to your interactions with your spouse. These fifteen skills fall under what experts call "active listening skills," and they are crucial if you are going to go from a relatively poor listener to a good one.

1. Listen with the Intent to Understand

We often get into conversations not really intending to understand what our spouse is saying, often waiting our turn until we can talk so they will listen to us. We need to set our minds on understanding what our spouse says before we respond. How are you doing when it comes to beginning conversations with the intention of understanding their feelings and point of view?

2. Repeat Back What You Heard

We filter what our spouse says through our own life experiences, blind spots, biases, and prejudices, something that can lead to a distorted understanding of what they are thinking and feeling. It is important to repeat back to our spouse what we heard them say so they can verify, tweak, or make major alterations to what we heard them say. How are you doing when it comes to repeating back to your spouse what you hear them say?

3. Keep Distractions to a Minimum

Make sure you are listening to your spouse in an environment that is relatively free from distractions. Turn your cell phone, television, and computer off so you can give them your full, undivided attention. And if you are internally distracted by something (personal problems, stress, difficult challenges), admit that to your spouse and see if you might talk later on so you can focus on what he or she is trying to say. How are you doing when it comes to keeping external and internal distractions to a minimum when listening to your spouse?

4. Maintain Good Eye Contact

Far too often, we are not looking into our spouse's eyes when we are listening to them. It has been said that the eyes are the window to the soul, so it is important to maintain good eye contact when communicating with our spouse. How are you doing when it comes to making good eye contact when you are interacting with your spouse?

5. Use Interruptions Sparingly

Conversations that do not go well are often marked by spouses interrupting and talking over one another. If we are going to interrupt, it needs to be for the purpose of clarifying what our spouse is saying or getting them to go more deeply into their thoughts and feelings. How are you doing when it comes to interrupting your spouse? Do you do it too much? When you do it, are you trying to clarify what your spouse is saying and get them to go into greater depth, or are you wanting to disagree or talk over them?

6. Lean In Rather Than Lean Back

Body language is important when you are conversing with your spouse. Leaning too far back says you are not all that interested in what they are saying. Leaning too far forward says you do not respect their personal space and are being invasive. While there is no magic formula, try to lean in to a reasonable degree when talking to your spouse. How are you doing when it comes to appropriately leaning in when talking to your spouse?

7. Put Yourself in Your Spouse's Shoes

If you want to truly understand your spouse, you have to have empathy and compassion about what they are going through. We must feel our spouse's pain in life; otherwise, we are not going to offer them very much in terms of love and understanding. How are you doing when it comes to having empathy and compassion for the pain and suffering your spouse experiences?

____

____

____

____

____

8. Be Curious

It is important when you are listening to your spouse that you exhibit curiosity about who they are, their life experiences, and how those things have shaped them. People are quite complex and nuanced, and if you are going to listen to your spouse well, you must approach them as an interpersonal Sherlock Holmes, trying to understand them in the deepest way possible. Curiosity may have killed the cat, but it is indispensable when we are trying to get to know our spouse better and more empathically. How are you doing when it comes to being curious about your spouse's inner world?

____

____

____

____

9. Suspend Judgment

If you really want to listen to your spouse and better understand where they are coming from, you must suspend judgment while you are listening. I am not suggesting you throw out your morals and core values in life, but you must be careful not to sit there in judgment of your spouse when you are trying to deeply understand them. Just try to accept what they are saying at face value as the way they view things, and refrain from making any statements that suggest you are judging them or their worldview. How are you doing when it comes to suspending judgment when you are listening to your spouse?

10. Give Up the Need to Be Right

A major reason conversations between spouses can take a turn for the worse is the human (but fallen) need to be right. Very few things will kill a conversation faster than either spouse trying to prove the other wrong. Do not make conversations with your spouse a competition—put aside your need to be right, listen deeply, and see if you can help both of you win by listening to and understanding each other. How are you doing when it comes to needing to be right in your interactions with your spouse?

11. Ask Clarifying Questions

To communicate that we are listening, we need to ask questions that demonstrate our desire to make sure we are hearing what our spouse is saying. Because we are prone to making assumptions, we need to ask our spouse to clarify what they are trying to tell us. How are you doing when it comes to asking questions that clarify what your spouse is trying to say?

12. Listen for Tone and the Words Not Being Said

When your spouse speaks, they speak with a certain tone and are editing themselves as they go. In your interactions with them, it is important to listen for the tone in their words and try to listen for the words they might not be saying. How are you doing when it comes to listening to your spouse's tone and picking up on what they are *not* saying to you?

13. Listen for the Ideas and Meanings underneath Their Words

While it is important to listen to the words your spouse says, it is even more important to hear the ideas and meanings underneath their words. Most of us struggle to speak words that capture the deeper ideas and values we hold. To be a good listener, we need to listen for the important "big picture" ideas our spouse is trying to express. How are you doing when it comes to listening for the bigger ideas behind your spouse's words?

14. Paraphrase

Sometimes it is enough to repeat what your spouse says. There are times, though, that we need to go beyond repeating ("parroting") their words and paraphrase what they said in a way that goes beyond their words. Do not worry about being wrong and misreading what your spouse is trying to tell you—they will appreciate that you were trying to listen so deeply that you would risk adding more nuance and depth to their words. How are you doing when it comes to paraphrasing what your spouse says and adding more to what their words suggest?

15. Ask Open-Ended Questions That Cannot Be Answered with a "Yes" or a "No"

There is a difference between asking your spouse, "Do you think changes should be made around here?" and "What changes would you make around here if you could?" Open-ended questions facilitate the depth of a conversation, whereas yes/no questions tend to truncate conversations. How are you doing when it comes to asking your spouse open-ended questions?

As you can tell from this rather extensive list, there is a lot that goes into being an effective listener. That is why we must roll up our sleeves and work on it with our spouse. You have heard the quote, "God gave us two ears and one mouth because he wants us to listen more than we talk." There is a lot of truth to that. Even if we listen more than we speak, we need to keep trying to raise our game and become even more effective listeners in our efforts to understand and have empathy for our spouse.

Becoming a good listener sets the stage for being able to speak the truth in love to your spouse when it is a healthy time to do so. I encourage you to resist giving your spouse feedback until you have practiced these active listening skills with them. If you do that, your input will be more accurate and loving.

If you want to get better at actively listening to your spouse and speaking the truth in love at a higher level, please consider reading the books listed below.

Recommended Reading

Crucial Conversations: Tools for Talking When Stakes Are High by Kerry Patterson, Joseph Grenny, Ron McMillan, Al Switzler, and Emily Gregory

I Hear You: The Surprisingly Simple Skill behind Extraordinary Relationships by Michael Sorensen

Just Listen: Discover the Secret to Getting Through to Absolutely Anyone by Mark Goulston

The Lost Art of Listening: How Learning to Listen Can Improve Relationships by Michael Nichols

You're Not Listening: What You're Missing and Why It Matters by Kate Murphy

LESSON NINE

Wiping the Slate Clean

We all harbor some degree of resentment and bitterness toward others. Unfortunately, that sometimes includes our spouse. When you are around someone 24/7, they are going to hurt you, and you are going to hurt them as well. The issue in marriage is not "Is my spouse going to wound me?" The issue in every marriage is "Am I going to forgive my spouse when they hurt me?"

Before we go any further, I want to remind you there are *no legitimate reasons* to withhold forgiveness from your spouse, only illegitimate ones. The *illegitimate reasons* we do not forgive our spouse for hurting us include: 1) falsely believing they have to earn your forgiveness for hurting you by changing their ways; 2) the possibility they are going to hurt you again; 3) they are not sorry or genuinely remorseful about what they have done; 4) the erroneous notion that you have to let the person who hurt you back into your life if you forgive them; 5) falsely believing that forgiving your spouse means what they did is not a big deal; and 6) falsely believing that forgiving your spouse means you are letting them get away with what they did.

Given there are no legitimate reasons to withhold forgiveness from your spouse for hurting you, let me offer you some legitimate reasons for forgiving them: 1) God commands it (Eph. 4:32); 2) you set yourself free from all the toxic emotions generated by unforgiveness (bitterness, resentment, and contempt, to name a few); 3) forgiving your spouse allows the emotional wound they inflicted to heal so you can put the past behind you; 4) it restores your relationship with God in that we cannot have a close relationship with him if we are carrying around bitterness, resentment, and unforgiveness toward others; 5) it serves as a good example to those around us, possibly inspiring them to do the same; 6) it allows God to work in your spouse's life when you quit presuming to be their judge, jury, and executioner; 7) it opens the door to reconciliation with your spouse, given that you are not holding things against them; 8) you are following the example of Christ, who was forgiving toward all those who wounded him (whether or not they were sorry or changed their ways); 9) it removes us from the victim chair and from presuming to punish them for what they did; and 10) forgiving our spouse enables us to experience the peace of Christ and opens the door to God's blessings in life.

I want you to work on forgiving your spouse (if you have not already) for the *major things* they have done to hurt you. I say "major things" because we do not need to forgive our spouse for the hundreds of minor ways they hurt us (examples: not being a very good listener, showing up late for a date, borrowing our stuff without asking, being inconsiderate). I am not minimizing these smaller "wounds" in marriage, but they do not rise to the level of major sins that we need to forgive.

Thirteen Steps to Forgiving Your Spouse

Considering the possibility your spouse has hurt you in significant ways in the marriage, I want you to choose one especially painful wound you experienced that you have not forgiven yet and run it through the steps below.

Step 1: *Acknowledge what your spouse did that hurt you.*

____

____

____

Step 2: *Recall the mental and emotional pain you experienced about what your spouse did.*

Step 3: *Acknowledge what your spouse did was wrong and that it is appropriate for you to feel hurt and angry about it.*

Step 4: *Hold your spouse fully responsible for what they did, even if it was in reaction to something you did that was hurtful to them.*

Step 5: *Acknowledge what your spouse did was not personal (it was about them, not you).*

Step 6: *Have compassion and empathy for your spouse that, like you, they are a deeply fallen human being.*

Step 7: *Remember the times you have been hurtful to your spouse, even if it was not to the same degree.*

Step 8: *Remember what it felt like in the past when others forgave you for hurting them.*

Step 9: *Allow the natural consequences of what your spouse did to come their way (breaking trust in the marriage, damaging their reputation in the community, getting fired from their job, being arrested).*

Step 10: *Consciously forgive your spouse for what they did (wipe the slate clean when it comes to holding it against them and give up your right to hurt them back).*

Step 11: *Hold on to forgiveness when tempted to take it back by reminding yourself you have already forgiven your spouse.*

Step 12: *Ask God to help you continue to forgive your spouse in the weeks and months to come (forgiveness is not a one-time act but something we need to do over and over).*

Step 13: *Pray for your spouse (for their growth toward becoming a more loving, mature, caring, and safe human being in their relationship with you).*

Deep marital wounds are hard to forgive, especially when your spouse does not take responsibility for what they did or seem to care that they hurt you. If you want to experience a better marriage, you need to forgive your spouse when they hurt you *no matter what*. You must make a commitment to stop poisoning your own soul by holding on to the resentment and bitterness that accompany unforgiveness. At the same time, you must keep your boundaries firmly in place and not attempt to reconcile until your spouse is willing to change their ways.

For any marriage to heal from a major marital wound, it takes two things. First, the spouse who inflicted the wound must be sorry and make amends. Second, the spouse who was wounded must be willing to forgive. If both spouses do their part, God can help any marriage survive even the most painful wounds and come out on the other side stronger and healthier than before.

If you want to get better at forgiving your spouse, please consider reading the books listed on the next page.

Recommended Reading

Forgive for Good: A Proven Prescription for Health and Happiness by Fred Luskin

Forgiving and Reconciling: Bridges to Wholeness and Hope by Everett Worthington

Forgiving What You Can't Forget: Discover How to Move On, Make Peace with Painful Memories, and Create a Life That's Beautiful Again by Lysa Terkeurst

Forgiveness Is a Choice: A Step-by-Step Process for Resolving Anger and Restoring Hope by Robert Enright

How to Forgive Ourselves Totally: Begin Again by Breaking Free from Past Mistakes by R. T. Kendall

I Want to Move On: Break Free from Bitterness and Discover Freedom in Forgiveness by Lauren Vander Linden

The Art of Forgiving: When You Need to Forgive and Don't Know How by Lewis Smedes

LESSON TEN

Telling on Yourself

Shame is a major issue for approximately 99.99 percent of the people on the planet. While it shows itself in many ways, one of the most destructive is that it can lead us to hide our flaws, defects, and struggles from the one we love. This, in turn, gets in the way of our relationship with that person being genuine, transparent, and intimate. This is especially true in marriage.

We counselors often use the phrase, "You are only as sick as your secrets," and it is not uncommon for spouses to keep a lot of things secret from one another. That pattern leads to guilt and shame in both spouses, something that gets in the way of the relationship being built on transparency and self-disclosure that could unite rather than divide a couple.

We are told in the Bible to "confess your sins to each other and pray for each other so that you may be healed" (James 5:16), and we would be wise to obey that principle in marriage so our marriages can be healed. At the same time, we need to be wise and discerning when it comes to what we confess to our spouse, as opposed to what we confess to safe, trustworthy counselors, pastors, and friends. Not every struggle we have or sin we commit should be confessed to our spouse, and we need to ask God to help us wisely choose what we confess to them as opposed to what we confess to trustworthy others.

One simple way to determine what to tell your spouse is to ask yourself, "Would my spouse be able to handle this information or would it be too upsetting to them if I shared it?" Here, you are having to humbly assess how spiritually and psychologically strong you perceive your spouse to be in hearing about your struggles, not something to be done lightly. Nevertheless, ask yourself this question before you share anything with them. If you feel sharing certain struggles with your spouse would be too upsetting to them, please consider sharing those struggle with someone else.

With that in mind, I want to run you through a series of questions to help you clarify your intentions in this area of your marriage. This will be a little disjointed at first, but I hope to pull it together for you by the end of the lesson.

What struggles and misdeeds are you hiding from your spouse that would be appropriate to tell them?

#1: ______________________________

____

____

#2: ______________________________

____

____

#3: ______________________________

____

____

What struggles and misdeeds are you hiding from your spouse that would *not* be appropriate to tell them?

#1: ______________________________

____

____

#2: ______________________________

____

____

#3: ______________________________

____

____

What has been the emotional and interpersonal cost of keeping these things to yourself?

____

____

____

____

____

What are some of the reasons you have kept these things from your spouse and others? These could include shame, pride, not being ready to stop, worry you will go back to the same bad behavior even after you tell your spouse about it, not wanting your spouse or others to think they are better than you, not wanting to be held accountable for changing your ways, and so on.

Go back to your spouse for a minute. Are you willing to talk with them about the need for healthy and appropriate confession of misdeeds to one another in the marriage and see if they will join you in this effort? If not, why not?

If you and your spouse are willing to do this, talk to each other about what level of specificity you are both willing to go to in confessing your wrong-doings and struggles to each other.

If the previous discussion stirs up too much contention and distress in the marriage, consider seeking counsel from a pastor, counselor, or mature person of faith to help you develop guidelines in this area of your marriage. Does anyone come to mind?

This is a risky area of marriage, to be sure. If we *appropriately* confess certain struggles and wrongdoings to our spouse, that information could be weaponized against us and cause great harm. If that is what you experience in your marriage, you need to seek marriage counseling so your counselor can help you work on why this is the case. We need to be safe in marriage to share many of the struggles we have as we go through life. If we are not safe, the marriage is unhealthy and needs outside help.

Whether it is with our spouse or someone else, we need to break free from the shame that keeps us hiding who we really are from others. We are only as sick as our secrets, and we need to identify those people we can safely share our struggles with so we can experience greater emotional and interpersonal health as we go through life.

If you want to get better at appropriately sharing your struggles with your spouse and other safe people, please consider reading the books listed on the next page.

Recommended Reading

A Small Book about Why We Hide: How Jesus Rescues Us from Insecurity, Regret, Failure, and Shame by Edward Welch

Daring Greatly: How the Courage to Be Vulnerable Transforms the Way We Live, Love, Parent, and Lead by Brené Brown

Shame and Grace: Healing the Shame We Don't Deserve by Lewis Smedes

Shame Interrupted: How God Lifts the Pain of Worthlessness and Rejection by Edward Welch

The Power of Vulnerability: Teachings of Authenticity, Connection and Courage by Brené Brown

The Soul of Shame: Retelling the Stories We Believe about Ourselves by Curt Thompson

LESSON ELEVEN

Having Compassion

Empathy is the ability to walk in someone else's shoes and feel their pain. Compassion involves taking positive steps to help alleviate a person's suffering. To develop a thriving marriage, we need to offer greater levels of both to our spouse as we live our lives together.

Most of us grew up hearing the story of the Good Samaritan. I would argue that the Good Samaritan had both empathy and compassion for the man he came across who had been brutally beaten and robbed. The Good Samaritan was not only able to empathize with the physical and emotional pain the victim was in, but he also took positive action to make sure this man was nursed back to health, expressing compassion in the process.

Had the Good Samaritan only felt empathy, he would have walked by the man like two others had done. It was the combination of empathy and compassion that led the Good Samaritan to express such a beautiful act of kindness, one that has reverberated through the ages as a lesson for us all.

The first thing I want to do in this lesson is walk you through the various components of how to develop greater empathy and compassion toward your spouse. Some of these ideas may strike you as silly or not worth doing, but I want you to consider them anyway. In the space provided, write down your thoughts about how you can put each of these ideas into action in your marriage.

Work on Active Listening

In an earlier chapter and workbook lesson, we explored that to have a healthier marriage we need to get better at active listening. Go back to the list in that lesson and write down which of the active listening skills you find the easiest to do and which ones you have the hardest time doing in your marriage.

____

____

____

____

____

Avoid Criticizing

To have more empathy and compassion toward your spouse, you must stop criticizing them. Write down some of the ways you find yourself being critical of your spouse as a person rather than critical of their wrong actions.

____

____

____

____

____

Discover Commonalities

Write down the things you have in common with your spouse (personality traits, life experiences, struggles, interests, hobbies, dreams, etc.). If we are going to have empathy and compassion for our spouse, it is important to see the ways we are similar and not camp out on how we are different.

Walk in Their Shoes

Set aside some time to think about what your spouse's life is like. Try to think through what a typical day for them is like, with all the plusses and minuses of their day-to-day experiences. Try to think through how the way they were raised may have wounded them. Write down what you were able to come up with in terms of empathizing with how things are for them.

Examine Your Biases and Prejudices

Take some time to think about any biases or prejudices you might have about your spouse that get in the way of having a closer relationship. Try to be unflinchingly honest about what your prejudices or biases are toward this person. Write them down below.

____

____

____

____

____

Be Curious and Ask Better Questions

Set aside time each week with your spouse to express greater curiosity about their life. Ask them to go into more detail about their life story, challenges they have overcome, hopes and dreams they have about their future, and the more troubling things that go through their soul each day. Write down what you learned about your spouse that you did not know before.

____

____

____

____

____

We all need to develop greater empathy and compassion toward our spouse. I encourage you to seriously consider making the things we explored in this section a regular part of your marriage so your ability to empathically and compassionately walk in your spouse's shoes can grow and develop over time.

If you would like to grow in having more compassion and empathy toward your spouse, please consider reading the books listed below.

Recommended Reading

Born for Love: Why Empathy Is Essential—and Endangered by Bruce Perry and Maia Szalavitz

Self-Compassion: Stop Beating Yoruself Up and Leave Insecurity Behind by Kristin Neff

Tattoos on the Heart: The Power of Boundless Compassion by Gregory Boyle

The Mindful Self-Compassion Workbook: A Proven Way to Accept Yourself, Build Inner Strength, and Thrive by Kristin Neff and Christopher Germer

The War for Kindness: Building Empathy in a Fractured World by Jamil Zaki

You, Me and Empathy: Teaching Children about Empathy, Feelings, Kindness, Compassion, Tolerance, Respect and Recognizing Bullying Behaviors by Janeen Sanders and Sofia Cardoso

LESSON TWELVE

Persevering through Thick and Thin, Especially the Thin

Marriage is hard work, and there are times we get discouraged and want to quit. The divorce rate is astronomically high, even among Christians, and that ought to tell us how hard it is to stay committed to our spouse "for better or for worse, through sickness and in health."

I say this to challenge you to persevere in your marriage, to not throw in the towel and walk away. Marriage is a gift from God, and we are to stay committed to our spouse in working out our marital salvation over time.

With this in mind, I want to take you back to the acronym PERSEVERANCE and ask you to write down your thoughts about whether you are willing to commit to each aspect of persevering in your marriage. Going letter by letter, you will write down what you are willing to do to persevere in growing closer over the rest of your lives.

Persevering in Your Marriage

If you and your spouse are committed to being married through thick and thin, make that more concrete by responding to the following aspects of perseverance. Only write down the things you are actually *willing* to do, not the things you *intend* to do. As they say, "The road to hell is paved with good intentions." I would say, "The road to marital hell is paved with good intentions," so only write down the things you are going to act on. Here we go.

Patience: Are you willing to be patient in allowing your marriage to mature over time, or are you going to leave it if things do not change fast enough?

Endurance: Are you willing to bear the pain of how hard marriage is, or are you going to seek instant gratification outside the marriage?

Resilience: Are you willing to bounce back up when you experience a painful marital setback, or are you going to stay down for the count when your marriage goes through a difficult time?

Sacrifice: Are you willing to sacrifice some of your own desires and aspirations to have a healthy marriage, or are you not wanting to have to give anything up to make your marriage work?

Effort: Are you willing put in the time and effort building a healthy marriage requires, or are you going to cut corners and not give it your all?

Vision: Do you have a biblical vision for what your marriage is all about (to help each other mature into fully loving human beings who can develop a healthy attachment)? Or are you struggling with an unbiblical vision for what you want out of your marriage (to be happy, to have all your needs met, to never have any conflict)?

Experience: Are you willing to learn from your mistakes along the way, or are you expecting you and your spouse to not make any mistakes and not have to learn and grow along the way?

Relationships: Are you willing to involve others in your efforts to have a healthy marriage (other couples, teachers, counselors, authors), or are you trying to do this alone as a couple?

Attitude: Are you willing to have a realistic attitude about marriage in terms of what you want from it, or are you still holding on to unrealistic, worldly attitudes about how smooth and easy marriage is supposed to be?

Necessity: Are you willing to do whatever it takes, within healthy moral constraints, to make your marriage better (meet with other couples, read books on marriage, get into counseling, attend marital retreats), or are you cutting corners on what you need to do to have the kind of marriage that is possible with God's help?

Courage: Are you willing to exhibit courage in your marriage (honestly face your own flaws and defects, let people give you feedback, improve your attachment style, love your spouse the way they need to be loved)?

Or are you going to play it safe and not go outside your comfort zone in doing what it takes to improve your marriage?

____

____

____

____

____

Enthusiasm: Are you willing to bring energy and excitement to your marriage each day, or are you going to be complacent and lethargic about the daily effort it takes to develop a thriving marriage?

____

____

____

____

____

You do not need me to tell you that having perseverance in marriage is easier said than done. Each one of the twelve aspects of perseverance we just covered is hard to do in and of itself, much less to work on doing all twelve at the same time. Nevertheless, God asks us to do all twelve and is ready, willing, and able to empower our efforts to do so.

If you have reached this point in the book, you have already demonstrated an ability to persevere in your marriage. I want to pat you on the back for that. Well done, good and faithful spouse! You have done something pleasing to God, loving toward your spouse, and good for your family heading into the future. I hope and pray you will spend the rest of your life co-laboring with your spouse to build a loving, healthy, and mature marriage that brings glory to God and gives future generations something to aspire to create in their own marriages.

If you want to get better at persevering in your marriage, please consider reading the books listed below.

Recommended Reading

Atomic Habits: An Easy & Proven Way to Build Good Habits & Break Bad Ones by James Clear

Grit: The Power of Passion and Perseverance by Angela Duckworth

How People Grow: What the Bible Reveals about Personal Growth by Henry Cloud and John Townsend

The Obstacle Is the Way: The Timeless Art of Turning Trials into Triumph by Ryan Holiday

Small Group Discussion Guide

I wrote this book hoping it would be used by couples in small group settings. This guide will help couples discuss the chapters and develop a greater sense of community.

The best way to lead a small group through *Real Marriage Made Simple* is to have everyone prepare by reading one chapter each week. Also, each couple should commit to working individually on the workbook lesson for each chapter. When the group meets, the leader can use the small group discussion guide to review and begin a discussion of the chapter. Some Scripture references are included in the study guide that the group can reflect on. Depending on your group dynamics, you may find it helpful to read these short Scriptures together. It is always a good idea to end group sessions with prayer.

Leading a small group on how to have a healthy and loving marriage can be challenging. I encourage you not to presume to be a therapist for any of the couples in the group, only their friend and fellow struggler in the pursuit of a loving marriage. If any of the couples in your group are struggling with deep levels of marital discord, encourage them to get couples counseling with a trained professional.

Confidentiality is important in this type of small group. Encourage everyone to be especially careful about what they share when it comes to their marriage, clearing confidences with their spouse before sharing them with the group. As you go through your meetings, if you feel anyone is not being careful or discerning in what they share, the group's leader should lovingly pull them aside and offer constructive feedback. If they are unwilling to listen, you may need to ask them to leave the group and seek counseling with a professional.

We need these relationships if our marriages are going to remain strong. May God bless you richly as you take on the challenge of strengthening your own marriage and helping others to grow in their relationships.

CHAPTER ONE—CAN'T WE JUST GET ALONG?

1. What is the first emotion that comes to mind when you think about improving your marriage? Why?

2. Does it make you uncomfortable to think about your own flaws or the flaws of your spouse? Why or why not?

3. Which of the core principles of a thriving marriage surprised you? Why?

4. Why is it important to comply with the core principles of relationships if we want to have a thriving marriage?

Scriptures to Consider

Matthew 7:3–5

1. What is hypocrisy and why does Jesus call it out?

2. In what ways is hypocrisy dangerous to a marriage?

3. Which items in the self-assessment are easiest to talk about? Which ones are more difficult?

James 2:1–4, 12–15

1. Why is favoritism so damaging to faith?

2. Why does mercy triumph over judgment?

Prayer: As a group, pray for each other as we begin this journey, that we can be honest with ourselves and that our marriages can grow.

CHAPTER TWO—STAY IN YOUR OWN BACKYARD

1. Recall and share a story in which your family got into a minor argument. What was at issue? Did anyone have particular trouble staying in their own backyard? In what ways did the argument escalate?

2. In the chapter story, Ben and Sally fight about money and spending habits. Do you relate to their struggle?

3. Dr. Thurman suggests in the chapter that when a person focuses on their spouse's issues, that person may be avoiding or running from issues in their own life. Do you think this is true? Why or why not?

4. How does it feel when your spouse is in your backyard rather than staying in their own?

5. How does your spouse feel when you are in their backyard rather than staying in your own?

Scriptures to Consider

Philippians 2:14

1. What happens to our spirit when we grumble and complain against others?

2. What should we do instead?

Ephesians 4:31

1. The apostle Paul encourages us to identify bitterness, rage, anger, brawling, slander, and malice. How do each of these complex emotions or actions make it more difficult to stay in our own backyard?

2. Each of the items in Paul's list can be difficult to manage. Which ones are a challenge for you and why?

Pray that in our marriages we can become more self-aware about the impact of our complaining and how this behavior might keep us from knowing ourselves better.

CHAPTER THREE—OWN YOUR OWN STUFF

This chapter describes two kinds of spousal blame games: *those who take too much responsibility* and *those who take too little.*

1. In the chapter, Jack blamed Debbie for making his life miserable. Debbie, in turn, blamed Jack. What damage did these actions do to their relationship?

2. Dr. Thurman suggests that a person who takes too little responsibility is character disordered. Would you agree or disagree and why?

3. When someone is overly responsible—taking more responsibility than they should—why is this a neurotic behavior? Where is the line of responsibility for our feelings and actions?

4. Why is blaming your feelings and actions on your spouse or allowing them to blame their feelings and actions on you damaging to a marriage?

Scripture to Consider

Psalm 139:23-24

1. What is the first emotion that comes to mind as you consider asking God to search your heart?

2. Do you worry about God being angry or disappointed with you? Is there something crucial that you're avoiding when you refuse to give God permission to search your heart?

3. Do you believe that you could experience a victory of owning your own stuff once you give God permission to examine your heart?

Pray for each other, knowing that confession leads to healing (James 5:16).

CHAPTER FOUR—GIVE MORE THAN YOU TAKE

1. What are the top emotional concerns that you can discern from the story of Beth and Sam?

2. Do you relate to any of these concerns?

3. Take a few minutes to break into couples and discuss the emotional needs in your marriages. Allow each spouse to name what they think are their top three emotional needs.

4. Are there particular emotional needs you are good at meeting in your spouse?

5. Are there particular emotional needs you are poor at meeting in your spouse?

Scripture to Consider
Romans 12:1

1. How can you offer yourself as a living sacrifice for others? How can you be an active agent of peace and support in your home?

2. Our activity is to be done "in view of God's mercy." How has God been merciful to you?

Pray that we can give to others as God has given to us (freely, lovingly, and for our good).

CHAPTER FIVE—HUMBLE YOURSELF

1. Finish the following phrases:

- Humility is when a person . . .
- The exact opposite of humility is ____________________ because ____.

2. Where in your marriage do you think too highly of yourself? Too lowly of yourself?

3. What flaws in your marriage do you have a hard time admitting to and overcoming?

4. What strengths do you bring to your marriage that you have a hard time giving yourself credit for?

Scriptures to Consider

1 Peter 5:5 and Psalm 51:17

1. What are the easiest ways that we can cultivate humility in our lives?

2. What are the chief obstacles that will prevent the growth of this virtue?

3. What is the connection between humility and salvation?

Take time in your group meeting to ask the couples to share their workbook answers, especially the fifteen ways to practice humility.

Pray that we willingly clothe ourselves with humility.

CHAPTER SIX—GET YOUR MIND RIGHT

1. In this chapter, Allen and Mary Beth struggled with the idea of entitlement. How did this idea damage their relationship?

2. Of the lies couples believe that we explored, which two or three do you struggle with?

3. Of the lies couples believe that you struggle with, what is the truth about those lies?

4. Why is believing the truth so important in marriage?

Scriptures to Consider

Ephesians 4:25 and Psalm 52:3

1. What happens to our relationships with each other if we love falsehood rather than the truth?

2. Why is God adamant that we speak truthfully?

3. What things do you need to do on a regular basis to renew your mind in marriage?

Pray that we become people who love truth.

CHAPTER SEVEN—STOP TALKING TRASH

1. Verbal abuse can take many forms. Of the different types covered in this chapter, which two or three hurt you the most? Why?

2. Which forms of verbal abuse are most harmful to your spouse?

3. In general, how hard is it for you to speak words that build up and encourage your spouse?

4. In general, how do you feel when abusive words are spoken to you?

5. What makes verbal abuse so damaging to relationships?

Scripture to Consider

1 Corinthians 13:4–7

1. How can these words from Paul inspire you to be a blessing to your spouse?

2. If someone speaks to us in a dismissive or condescending way, how do we not keep a record of wrongs? What should we do if someone offends us?

Pray that we can minimize the harm caused by our words and find more ways to be creative in offering blessing.

CHAPTER EIGHT—SHOOT STRAIGHT FOR THEIR GOOD

1. When giving your spouse feedback about their behavior, how hard is it for you to be accurate?

2. When giving your spouse feedback, how hard is it for you to do it out of a loving heart?

3. How does it feel when you are being given feedback that is either inaccurate or mean-spirited, or both?

4. How do you think your spouse feels when you are giving them feedback that is either inaccurate or mean-spirited, or both?

Scripture to Consider

Ephesians 4:15

1. What does it mean to speak the truth in love?

2. How is it damaging if the truth is spoken with malice? Or indifference?

Pray for God's spirit to strengthen us to have marriages that are filled with kindness.

CHAPTER NINE—WIPE THE SLATE CLEAN

1. Focusing on the smaller hurts of marriage, which have you struggled to forgive?

2. Which of the *illegitimate* reasons for not forgiving your spouse do you struggle with?

3. Which of the legitimate reasons for forgiving your spouse do you struggle with?

4. When you fall into unforgiveness, what is the emotional and interpersonal cost?

Give couples time to talk about this chapter and share their workbook answers with each other.

Scripture to Consider

Luke 15:11–32

1. Why did the father accept his son back? Was it because he repented?

2. Why wouldn't the older brother attend the party?

3. Why did the father throw a party for the younger son?

Pray that we can forgive as we have been forgiven.

CHAPTER TEN—TELL ON YOURSELF

1. Ted and Cindy were having trouble because Ted was keeping secrets. Do you find their story believable? Why or why not?

2. How did shame play a role in why Ted kept secrets?

3. Have you been tempted to keep things from your spouse?

4. How do you feel when you keep these things from them?

5. Why does Dr. Thurman suggest that we are only as sick as our secrets?

Scripture to Consider

Psalm 139:1–4 and 1 John 4:7–8

1. The psalmist says that God knows us. Why is it good news that we can't keep secrets from God?

2. Is it loving to keep secrets?

Pray that we can have the courage to be vulnerable and loving.

CHAPTER ELEVEN—HAVE COMPASSION

1. What emotions come to mind when you think about showing compassion to your spouse?

2. How difficult has it been for you to have compassion for your spouse's struggles and challenges?

3. Of the active listening skills we covered, which ones do you have a hard time practicing in marriage?

4. Of the active listening skills we covered, which ones are relatively easy for you to do in marriage?

5. What is it like when your spouse listens to you in a deep and understanding way?

Scripture to Consider

Matthew 14:13–14

1. Jesus was grieving the execution of John the Baptist (Matt. 14:1–12), but crowds of people followed him. What was his response to their needs?

2. Was it out of the ordinary for Jesus to act in a compassionate way toward the crowds?

3. How does Jesus give us the power to act with compassion toward our spouse, family, coworkers, and others?

4. Is compassion always the right response?

Pray that we can grow in compassion and become more like Jesus.

CHAPTER TWELVE—PERSEVERE THROUGH THICK AND THIN, ESPECIALLY THE THIN

1. Of the twelve aspects of PERSEVERANCE we explored, which two or three do you struggle with in marriage?

2. Of the twelve aspects of PERSEVERANCE we explored, which two or three do you find easy to do in marriage?

3. When you find yourself growing weary of working on your marriage, what do you tend to do?

4. What are you doing to involve others in helping you to have a healthy, loving marriage?

Scripture to Consider

Galatians 6:1–10

1. How do these verses apply to your marriage?

2. What is compassion fatigue? Have you grown tired of doing good deeds?

3. Are there solutions suggested in this text for when we grow tired?

Pray for each other that we can be patient and persevere.

Acknowledgments

My thanks to Dr. Jason Fikes, Duane Anderson, Mary Hardegree, and all the wonderful people at Leafwood Publishers. You have been a pleasure to work with, and I will never be able to thank you enough for the expertise and professionalism you brought to this project.

Much appreciation to Mark and Marj McClain, Joel and Stacy Hock, and Todd and Kathy Cox. Your gracious support considerably lightened my load as an author and made it possible to find a wonderful publisher to collaborate with me in getting this book into print.

Thanks to all the couples I have been blessed to work with over the years. It has been a privilege to pull up alongside as you courageously work on making your marriage all that God wants it to be, and I greatly appreciate you allowing me into your lives.

Heartfelt gratitude to my wife, Holly. You have been a constant source of grace and kindness over the five decades we have been married. Proverbs 31:10 says, "A wife of noble character who can find? She is worth far more than rubies." God blessed me with such a wife when I found you, and I am eternally grateful for how loving you have been over the years.

And, finally, my deepest thanks to God. How do you properly thank God, someone who loves you unconditionally, saved you from your lostness, adopted you into his family, and looked out for you throughout your life? Truth be told, you cannot. God, thank you for loving me the extravagant way you do, with no strings attached, and patiently teaching me how to love you and my neighbor in return.

About the Author

Dr. Chris Thurman is a psychologist, author, and popular speaker. Chris has authored numerous books, including the bestseller *The Lies We Believe*. He has conducted hundreds of personal growth seminars for churches and corporations around the country. Chris and his wife, Holly, have been married for forty-four years and have three grown children and three grandchildren they think hung the moon.

For more information on bringing Chris to speak to your church or company, please feel free to contact him at www.drchristhurman.com.

Books by Dr. Chris Thurman

Emotionally Healthy Christianity: Following in the Psychological Footsteps of Christ
If Christ Were Your Counselor
It's Your Attitude: Out with the Bad, In with the Good
The Lies Couples Believe: How Living the Truth Transforms Your Marriage
The Lies We Believe: Renew Your Mind and Transform Your Life, 30th Anniversary Edition
The Lies We Believe about God: Knowing God for Who He Really Is
The Lies We Believe Workbook: A Comprehensive Program for Renewing Your Mind and Transforming Your Life, Revised Edition
Pop's Advice: Godly Guidance for My Grandkids . . . and Everyone Else
Restoring Your Sanity: A Spiritual Path to Psychological Health
Self-Help or Self-Destruction? Ten Pop Psychology Myths That Could Destroy Your Life
Stop Shoulding All Over Yourself: Making the Journey from Condemnation to Compassion
The Truths We Must Believe: Twelve Timeless Principles for Confident Living